T0191423

TO UNIFY A NATION

My Vision for the Future of Israel

MK Rabbi

DOV LIPMAN

Foreword by Minister of Finance
MK YAIR LAPID

URIM PUBLICATIONS
Jerusalem • New York

To Unify a Nation: My Vision for the Future of Israel

by Dov Lipman

Copyright © 2014 by Dov Lipman

Printed in Israel

First Edition

ISBN 978-965-524-148-8

Urim Publications, P.O. Box 52287, Jerusalem 9152102 Israel

www.UrimPublications.com

Library of Congress Cataloging-in-Publication Data

Lipman, Dov Moshe.
  To unify a nation : my vision for the future of Israel / MK Rabbi Dov
Lipman ; foreword by Minister of Finance, Yair Lapid.
    pages   cm
  ISBN 978-965-524-148-8 (hardback)
  1. Judaism and state–Israel. 2. Religion and state–Israel. 3.
Jews–Identity. 4. Orthodox Judaism–Relations–Nontraditional Jews. I.
Title.
  BM538.S7L57 2014
  320.95694–dc23   2014000591

Dear Dov,

I want to thank you for sending me your book *To Unify a Nation*. You deserve appreciation for your activities which seek to build bridges of unity, understanding, and tolerance between the religious and non-religious populations in Israel. Your public actions serve as an example of responsible rabbinic work which adds honor to the Jewish nation and to the State of Israel and reflects the deep ethics and morals of Judaism in its glory.

With blessings of praise,
Shimon Peres

This book is dedicated in memory of our father

MENDEL FRIEDMAN,

who survived Auschwitz and Bergen-Belsen.

We wish our father had the privilege of living in a world

that exemplifies the values of tolerance and acceptance as

espoused in MK DOV LIPMAN's book.

We pray that such a world will exist

for our future generations.

⌘

MIRIAM FRIEDMAN ZUSSMAN
and NATHAN ZUSSMAN

MARTIN FRIEDMAN *and*
SUZANNE WALTMAN

Contents

Foreword by Finance Minister Yair Lapid

WHEN WE ASK OURSELVES what the difference is between successful and unsuccessful societies – the answer is the ability to adapt.

Successful societies know how to change and to adapt to changes around them while preserving the core that makes them unique. Tribes that did not make the transition from the Stone Age to the Bronze Age disappeared from our collective memories. Companies that were not able to advance from an agricultural economy to an industrial society collapsed. Countries that did not adapt from an industrial society to the hi-tech and social network-driven global environment in which we currently live were left behind.

The Jewish nation has and always had this ability. The nomadic tribes of Abraham, our forefather, became the nation of warriors led by King David. The group that was exiled – lost, with no chance to succeed – and then dispersed across the world after the destruction of the Second Temple, became the nation of the Talmud. Woodchoppers and water-drawers who left Eastern Europe and crossed the Atlantic Ocean became bankers, inventors, authors, entrepreneurs, politicians, and movie producers, and together were crucial contributors to the design of the new world.

The Jews who came to Israel also had this capacity to change. We always have the ability to reinvent ourselves. We did this in 1948 when a handful of Holocaust survivors learned how to take arms in one hand and a plow in the other, and built a State. We did this in the 1950s and again in the 1990s when a million immigrants flooded Israel and changed its demographics in nearly an instant. We did this in our transition from being the nation of the Talmud to the nation of the kibbutz, from the nation of the kibbutz to the nation of education, and from the nation of education to the start-up nation.

This part, the last one, we did very well. There is something in the Israeli DNA, in the narrative of the Jewish nation that is particularly suitable to the Information Age. The collective Jewish memory, which was formed and perfected through hundreds of years of Torah and Talmud study, looks at the information revolution and it all seems familiar – linking subjects to one another, grasping massive amounts of information, the ability to probe deeper and deeper in one area and continuously find new information. Knowledge is fluid and changes, gets erased, and is continuously rewritten again. My friend, Professor Emmanuel Trachtenberg, calls this "*vu ja du*," the opposite of "*de ja vu*." In other words, it is the ability to look at something and to see things within that no other person saw before you.

This ability will be put to a difficult test in the coming years. We live in a world in which everyone feels that he has the right to define himself, to himself, and by himself. This outlook, as enlightened as it may be, presents a difficult challenge for any human group that feels obligated to one founding ethos or to a joint narrative.

Because, what in essence binds Maimonides to Leonard, the legendary twentieth-century Jewish boxer? What do Albert Einstein and an Ethiopian Jew who immigrated to Israel by foot through the Sudan have in common? What connects Freud to Moses, our teacher? What links an assimilated Austro-Hungarian Jew named Theodor Herzl to a famous feminist like Betty Friedan other than the fact that they both wrote about the "problem that has no name?" What unites a brilliant, optimistic, and tireless Orthodox rabbi like Dov Lipman and . . . me? Are we telling the same story? Are we capable of agreeing about the past in order to work together to create a common future?

This book, much like its author, deals with this problem with courage and wisdom. This is not simply a book but a call to action and the beginning of a discussion.

To any knowledgeable Jew, it is clear that the connection between us is undergoing a deep change. We don't know what this change will be, but at least we know that we can change.

Acknowledgements

I AM WRITING THESE WORDS overwhelmed with feelings of gratitude. I am sitting at my desk in my Knesset office. "A song of ascents when God returns the captive Zion, we were like dreamers." This experience is nothing short of a dream. When my wife and I walked down the steps from that El Al flight with our four children, close to nine years ago, we could have never imagined the chain of events and decisions which led to my sitting in this chair today.

My first thank you goes to God. I recognize His hand in guiding me to this role and not only thank Him for the opportunity to serve His people and country in this capacity but beseech Him to assist me in making the difficult decisions and shouldering the responsibilities which have come my way.

Community work and responsibility for the Jewish people was modeled to me from the youngest of ages. My grandparents Marvin and Blanche Lipman, of blessed memory, and Rev. Avraham (OBM), and may she live and be well, Ethel Kleinman, dedicated their time and great energies on behalf of the Jewish people. My father, Judge Ronald Lipman, of blessed memory, managed to reach great heights professionally while also serving as a lay leader in our synagogue, schools, and other community organizations. My mother, Leah Lipman Zeiger, has always been involved in communal affairs and remains active together with her husband, Dr. Allen Zeiger. My father-and mother-in-law, Rabbi Moshe and Cheryl Abramowitz, raised their family on United States Army bases around the country and the world in dedication to providing religious services to Jewish soldiers. Everyone mentioned in this paragraph broke down barriers and helped unite the Jewish people by reaching out to help Jews of all backgrounds throughout their lives. I thank God for the example which all of them provided for me and my wife, Dena, as we strive to follow their example and for their love and support.

Dena and I have been blessed to raise our four children – Shlomo, Devora, Chaya Miriam, and Zahava in the Holy Land. There are no words to adequately thank Dena and all the children for all their support and patience as I made the transformation from innocent immigrant, to concerned citizen, to community activist, to political activist, to member of Knesset. We talk regularly about the need for unity and greater sanctification of God's name in Israel and we are truly a team.

This book is dedicated to the memory of my father, Ron Lipman, of blessed memory. It is difficult to comprehend that my father is not with me physically by my side through all that I am experiencing. While I miss him terribly, his example has accompanied me every step of the way. I find myself asking "What would Daddy do?" on a near daily basis. My father was a magnet for unity. Whether at his office, while walking down the street in our neighborhood, in our synagogue, or next to strangers at a ball game, he was the first to introduce himself, sincerely ask "How are you?" and demonstrate that people from all backgrounds can get along and be the best of friends if we simply make the effort.

I thank Miriam and Natan Zussman and Joel and Marni Eizikovitz for sponsoring this book. Thank you to Tzvi Mauer and the entire staff at Urim Publications for their professionalism throughout the project. They were an absolute pleasure. My chief of staff, Alisa Coleman, and my spokesman, Benjy Goldberg, play important roles in all that I do and this book is no exception. Thank you for your professionalism and dedication.

I must also thank Finance Minister Yair Lapid and all ministers, MKs, and administrators of the Yesh Atid party. You have welcomed me into the party with such warmth and we function in unity and as a family. We are working together to accomplish the goals outlined in this book and I thank you for this remarkable opportunity. A special thank you to Finance Minister Yair Lapid for writing an inspiring foreword and to President Shimon Peres and Natan Sharansky for taking the time to review the manuscript and write a letter of approbation.

People tell me that I am dreaming if I believe that we can create unity amongst the Jewish people in Israel. My response to those doubters is clear and to the point. Growing up in Silver Spring, Maryland, we used to take the short ride to Washington, DC a few times a year to demonstrate on behalf of Russian Jewry in front of the Soviet Embassy. During one of those protests, someone handed me a sign to hold up in silent demonstration. The sign read: "Free Yuli Edelstein." Today, decades later, I sit in the Knesset chamber as a member of the Israeli parliament and in the front of the room sits the speaker of the Knesset – Yuli Edelstein.

Dreams can come true. We just have to believe in ourselves and believe in man's capacity to accomplish the "impossible." King David wrote that in our return to Zion we are "like dreamers." Living in the Land of Israel is a dream. Preparing my fourth book for publication is a dream. My beautiful family is a dream. Serving as a member of the Knesset is a dream. I thank God for all the dreams in my life and pray for His assistance to achieve the difficult, but necessary, one described in this book – unifying our nation.

MK Rabbi Dov Lipman
Jerusalem, Israel
Kislev 5774 / November 2013

Introduction

IT WAS THE GREATEST moment of disillusionment in my life.

Having grown up in a religiously observant home and having received an education in religious schools, the focus of Judaism was Torah study, mitzvah observance, and prayer. But, aside from the rituals of daily religious life, my parents taught me core Jewish values which included respecting all people and always striving for unity. Having had close contact throughout my life with Jews of all backgrounds, I had always viewed the high levels of non-observance as the greatest internal threat to the future of our nation. I was mistaken.

I had the good fortune of immigrating to Israel with my wife and four children in July, 2004. Several months later, while sitting in my home, I heard a commotion in the street. I looked out the window and saw some police cars. I immediately went outside, heard people chanting something out their windows, and innocently asked a policeman what was happening. He replied, "Run, run, quickly, run." Before I had the chance to naively ask him why I should run, a hailstorm of rocks came flying at us from a nearby building and I was hit in the leg. Religious extremists were protesting some issue and in their disgust over the Israeli police presence they first chanted anti-police slogans and then threw rocks at them. And, at me.

At that moment, reality hit hard. A process began in which I realized that polarization caused by extremism and isolationism in the religious community may be the greatest internal threat to the future of the Jewish people. All of our classic sources and basic logic dictate that the key to our success as a nation is unity. When that rock hit my leg I realized that while religious practice always has and always will be central to my daily life and overall belief system, our greatest threat was not the lack of religious observance among Jews, but rather the abandonment of core Jewish values and ideals which include loving-kindness, respecting others, and not doing onto others what you don't want done to yourself.

I decided to try to help diffuse the tensions between those "rock throwers" and other populations. However, the more involved I became, the more I came to realize the depths of the extremism and isolationism, and the serious levels of abandonment of core Jewish values that came in its wake. Even more significantly, I began to notice the degree of polarization it caused. To be clear: The religious community is replete with wonderful people living their lives with beautiful values. However, because of the isolation, that beauty tends to stay within the community and is not projected outward. All that broader Israel sees is the extremism.

I thought about the devastating ramifications this type of extremism could have on the wide variety of Jews I had bonded with at various points in my life. What would the Ethiopian children with whom I sang and played ball at the Diplomat Hotel during their first few weeks in Israel think about an Israel in which Jews hated each other to this degree? My non-observant Israeli cousins, who I visited before the holidays while studying in yeshiva in Israel, showed signs of a lack of connection to Judaism. What role did religious Jews not acting with Jewish values play in my cousins' disenchantment with their heritage? I thought about the children who were campers in a summer camp in Tiblisi, Georgia where I served as counselor, who had since immigrated to Israel. Would they have any desire to begin the process of reconnecting to their heritage if they did not see the beauty of core Jewish values on display among their new neighbors in Israel? How deep is the despair among those who suffered as Jews in the Soviet Union because they had Jewish fathers and are now unwelcome in Israel because they don't have Jewish mothers? I thought about my non-Orthodox campers in the day camp where I worked in Frederick, Maryland who were certain to come to Israel on Birthright trips. Knowing them, they would be inspired by the degree of religious observance which surrounded them on these visits, but how many would be turned off because of negative encounters with those who externally appeared to be very religious?

Fast forward seven years.

It was one of the proudest moments of my life.

I was standing on a stage together with Jews from all backgrounds – moderate Haredi, Religious Zionist, traditional, non-observant, men, women, English-speaking immigrants as well as immigrants from Russia and Ethiopia. We all united to declare that we were against religious coercion, religious extremism, and violence. We were standing in front of thousands of people who came from all over Israel, as well as addressing a national television audience. We rallied together around these core principles and, in doing so, stood up to religious extremists who had been verbally assaulting young girls over what they deemed to be immodest dress. Despite our external differences

and our different beliefs and approaches to religious observance, while standing on that stage I felt a true kinship with
my fellow Jews who helped plan the rally and the thousands
of diverse individuals in the crowd. Our bond revolved around
basic Jewish values and not our shared religious practice.

I realized that not only did the abandonment of core Jewish
values, especially among some segments in religious circles,
lead to terrible disunity and polarization, but that those values
themselves are the only thing that can truly unify the Jewish
people. That realization ultimately led to my joining the Yesh
Atid party and proudly serving in the Israeli Parliament with
Yesh Atid MKs from all backgrounds and populations.

While we have no shortage of external foes who threaten our
future existence, I believe that the greatest threat to our future
is internal. Ignoring these core Jewish values, which should be
the unifying force among populations with differing cultures,
traditions, and levels of religious observance, will tear us apart
if not dealt with and confronted head-on.

The time has come for all Jews to re-embrace our core values
of respecting the rights of others and working together as a
people. To do so, we must combat the extremism, isolationism,
and indecency which threaten to polarize the Jewish people to
a point of no return. The time has come to unify as a people
and save our nation.

⇒ *One* ⇐

Dignity of Man

THE MOST BASIC of Jewish values, which cannot be over-emphasized in our schools, in our homes, in our community centers, and in our places of worship, is that all humans are created "in the image of God" and deserve to be respected as such. Throughout our tradition God is described as "merciful," "compassionate," and as a Being of loving-kindness. Through that lens, human beings are capable of the most remarkable "divine-like" behavior. This is not simply a statement at the outset of the Bible, but has been proven time and time again.

Rick Hoyt's brain was deprived of oxygen during his birth in 1962, resulting in living his life as a spastic quadriplegic with cerebral palsy. His parents, Dick and Judy, were told to "free" themselves by simply putting Rick into an institution since there was no hope for him to live a normal life. Despite seeing clearly that Rick could not speak or walk as he grew older, Dick and Judy noticed how Rick's eyes followed everything that was happening. They were convinced that his brain was processing what occurred around him and that he could enjoy various experiences.

Dick and Judy took Rick sledding and swimming and could sense his joy. They took this one step further and taught him the alphabet and basic words. They were convinced that their son comprehended everything and were desperate to find a way to enable him to communicate with them. When Rick was ten years old, they paid $5,000 to engineers at Tufts University to build an interactive computer for Rick. The computer lit up the letters of the alphabet, and when the letter that Rick wanted would light up, he tapped his head against the head piece of his wheelchair.

Dick and Judy's theory about their son's ability to understand was proven to be accurate when his first communication via the computer was "Go, Bruins," the hometown professional hockey team which was in the league championship that season. This made it clear to everyone that Rick loved sports and was able to be a fan like everyone else.

When Rick was 15, he told his father that he wanted to join a five-mile run on behalf of a lacrosse player who became paralyzed in an accident. Being an ever-dedicated father, Dick agreed to push Rick in his wheelchair, and they completed the race. That night, Rick told his father, "Dad, when I'm running, it feels like I'm not handicapped."

That was all Dick needed to hear. Dick dedicated his life to entering races with his son to maximize the amount of time Rick would feel not handicapped. They competed in over 1,000 races including marathons and triathlons. The triathlon includes swimming and biking. Dick swam with Rick in a boat attached by a bungee cord to a vest on Dick's waist. He rode a special two-seater bike with Rick in front.

This dedication of parent to child demonstrates the "God-like" capacities latent within all human beings.

A person could read this and think that this is merely a

special gift which enables people to have the capacity to give to their own children. Linda Elsass disproves this theory. In 1978, Elsass's son was dating a girl, Darlene, whose parents threw her out of the house and was labeled "incorrigible." The girl was required to appear in court with the possible outcome of being forced to live in an institution for troubled youth. Linda's son asked his mom to accompany Darlene to court since he had to be in school that day. She did so and someone in the court-room asked Linda about taking Darlene in as a foster child. She initially declined because she had her own children to care for. But then she thought about Darlene not having parents and decided she had to do it. The Elsasses took in Darlene and, as she relates, "It never stopped."

The family became known as the address for any children in need. Ultimately, Linda and her husband, Larry, played a role in raising 250 children, some of whom stayed for just a few hours, others for weeks, and many for months. As Larry com-mented, "When I went to work in the morning, I didn't know if I would have a place at the supper table when I got home. I started counting them when I got home to see who was new." Lest one think that these children did not receive adequate attention, one foster child, Dee Hoffman explained: "Before coming here, I had been in many foster homes, but when I got here, I knew this was home. They helped shape my life, and I never left. They are my mom and dad." The selflessness displayed by Linda can only be described as "Godly."

Lest anyone thinks that this type of giving is limited to par-ents and their children, biological or not, Tyler Kellog's story dispels that notion. Tyler was a 21-year old college student who decided that life should revolve around acts of kindness. He saved $2,000, equipped his car with a place to sleep, and set off to drive 2,600 miles from New York to Florida and back in order to "perform acts of kindness for strangers." During his trip he helped 115 individuals in varied circumstances. He helped a person get his boat into a lake, assisted a policeman in setting up a barricade, and spread mulch with gardeners. But the most meaningful moment came when he saw a man crying and he asked, as he always did, "Can I help you?" The man responded that his wife had recently died and he had no one to talk to. They sat for three hours and simply talked. When Tyler stood up to leave, the man said, "Thank you, I realize now that my life will go on." Yes, human beings are "Godly" and can give other people the ability to go on with their lives through the power of the simple words, "Can I help you?"

We should not make the mistake of thinking that only people who perform acts of kindness of significant magnitude, people like Dick Hoyt, Linda Elsass, and Tyler Kellog deserve the highest levels of respect. Everyone, regardless of stature or fame, incubates these remarkable qualities within themselves and can call up these resources even for small, perhaps mundane, circumstances that arise in life.

This idea became crystal clear to me personally when I was sitting *shiva* for my beloved father. He was a federal judge and a community leader and a continuous stream of friends sought to console my family in my parents' home in Silver Spring, Maryland for the week following his passing. One day, when the room was overflowing with visitors, the front door opened, and in walked our mailman, sobbing like a little child. People moved to the side as he approached my family, sitting in a row in the front of the room. He kneeled before my mother, handed her flowers, and while sobbing, with tears coursing down his face, he managed to say, "I am so sad that Judge Lipman passed away."

Why was our mailman so broken up over my father's death to the point that I had to console him?

I asked him about their relationship and he explained: "As a mailman, I spend my day delivering the mail without much contact with other people. Whenever your father was home, the moment he heard me putting the mail through the slot, he would come to the door, offer me a cold or hot drink, talk some sports with me and sincerely ask how I was doing. Whenever I began my day, I actually hoped that your Dad would be home. I am going to miss him so much."

What incredible capacity all humans have to touch the lives of others and literally make their day with the most simple of gestures.

This "Godly image" extends to our capacity to care for other species as well. In 1999, Danish conservationist Lone Droscher-Nielsen founded the Nyaru Menteng Orangutan Reintroduction Project in the jungles of Borneo, an island in Southeast Asia. She created this project to protect orangutans who were orphaned in their natural habitat between Borneo and Sunetra, an area which is being cleared for logging and oil palm plantations. She heard that the homeless orangutans would wander near villages to find food and were scared away by the locals. Surviving infants would cling to their dead mothers. She had to act.

This orangutan orphanage hires nurses to raise these animals as their own children, including feeding, cuddling, singing lullabies, and teaching them. The orangutans need this motherly love and the nurses are available for them 24 hours a day. Once the orangutans reach a mature age where they can protect themselves, they are released to the project's protected forest to live freely.

The Bible describes God as a Being who bestows life to everything on Earth (Nehemiah 9). As Lone's project demonstrates, human beings are blessed with this ability as well.

No one should suggest that certain humans have these special qualities while the murderers and criminals throughout world history do not.

The Talmud tells the story of Simeon the son of Lakish who lived 1,800 years ago in Palestina, the Roman province of Syria. Simeon was a gladiator in a circus where he fought with wild beasts. He then resorted to life as a bandit, robbing travelers while living in the wilderness. However, he turned his life around and emerged as one of the greatest Talmudic scholars and Jewish leaders of his time. The Talmud, no doubt, teaches us this story to demonstrate that everyone has the capacity for greatness if directed and guided in the right direction at the right time.

It may be difficult to relate to a story about some rabbi who lived nearly 2,000 years ago, and we may speculate that while this concept may have been true back then, it would be difficult to see "God's image" in a gang member involved in the worst crimes in the worst neighborhoods. Greg Mathis proves that this faith in human greatness applies even in modern times. At a young age, Mathis became associated with the notorious Errol Flynns street gang in Detroit, Michigan. After being released from prison after his incarceration at the age of 17, Greg turned his life around, eventually rising to become a federal judge and the star of the syndicated television show "Judge Mathis." His story became the inspiration for a play and a book called *Inner City Miracle*.

The great sage Hillel captures the essence of this ideal in *Ethics of Our Fathers* with just a few words: "Love all people." He doesn't say to love close family members, love close friends, love those who are acting in accordance with your beliefs, or love fellow Jews. He says love all people. While "loving" all people may be a difficult level to achieve, we can all certainly strive to, at the very least, respect all fellow human beings.

Every Passover, millions of Jews around the world demonstrate how far our respect for *all* humans reaches. We read the Haggadah, which relates the story of the Jewish people's enslavement in Egypt and the remarkable story of our exodus from there. As part of that story we recount the ten plagues which befell the Egyptians and ultimately led to their freeing the Jews. One would think that this would be the most satisfying part of the Seder. However, the custom to remove wine from our cups as we list the plagues reminds us to be sad over the deaths of our enemies! Yes, they persecuted us. Yes, they tortured us. Yes, they killed us. But they are human beings "in God's image" and we do not rejoice over their downfall, and wish the story could have had a happier ending for them. This idea is captured by the powerful words of King Solomon: "When your enemies fall, do not rejoice" (Proverbs 24:17). We may have to injure, or even kill, enemies who seek to harm or kill us. However, we are not happy about having to do so, and still respect their dignity as much as is possible.

Based on the above, attacks on mosques by extreme right-wing Jews, or the torching of Palestinian-owned fields, have no place in Judaism. The army must take action to protect Israeli citizens. But all attacks by the Israeli army are planned to avoid civilian casualties on the enemy side , and there is no gloating over those who we kill during these missions.

This core Jewish value is captured by a front cover headline in the November 25, 2007 *Washington Post* which said: "In his job as an Israeli pediatrician, Yuval saves the lives of Palestinian children. But the father of three also takes Palestinian lives as

an attack helicopter pilot patrolling Gaza." The article is about
Yuval, a major in the air force who lives on the Palmachim air
force base north of the Gaza Strip. He works in a nearby hos-
pital during the day, often treating Palestinian children from
Gaza, and flies a Cobra helicopter and fires at targets in the
Gaza Strip at night. To quote from the article regarding his
role as a pilot:

> When he's ordered to kill, "I try to think of it as I'm helping
> to save lives, and not hurting lives." In Gaza, flying over the
> orchard, he had killed two men, but let the other two go, he
> said. The risk of hitting civilians was too high.

Regarding also serving as a doctor treating Palestinian children,
the article explains:

> "My oath as a doctor is primo no nocere, do no harm," even
> if they are Palestinian children . . . It was sad for Yuval, but
> he often thought that the Gaza children had "a 90 percent
> chance of becoming terrorists. But mainly, it's not their fault,
> it's 'the situation's fault.' And I'm not treating 'the situation.'
> I'm treating the child."

Major Yuval serves as the perfect example of who we need to
emulate as Jews. He epitomizes the Jewish value of respect and
dignity to fellow humans, even toward enemies, and does so in
the most difficult of circumstances.

This concern for the respect of enemies, and even wicked
people, is rooted in our genes from our founding father,
Abraham. When he learns about the imminent destruction of
Sodom, he refuses to rest until he realizes that he could not do
anything about it (see Genesis Chapter 18). The example set
by Abraham, as well as the custom to spill wine at the Seder,
should serve as our guide regarding the respect and concern we

should have for all humans. The great Talmudic figure, Rabbi Yochanan ben Zakai, made a point of greeting every person he met in the marketplace. It made no difference if this person was a Jew, gentile, righteous, or wicked. Humans are humans and the most basic Jewish value is to respect every human as they are, and to treat them with basic dignity.

When I was younger, I had the great thrill to play varsity basketball and the honor of being named a first-team all-star in the Metropolitan International Basketball League in the greater Washington, DC area. This experience put me in contact with many non-Jewish players, opening my world beyond the experiences of the all-Jewish high school I attended. I struggled to reconcile the negative slant some of my Jewish religious teachers had towards non-Jews with what I saw and experienced in these non-Jewish players. They were devout, value-centered, and would rush to lend me a hand and help me to my feet when I fell during games.

As I thought about this as an adult, I came to understand that Jews around the world have been influenced, understandably, by 2,000 years of exile and horrific persecution. Distrust and an acceptance of acting without respect has become part of the Jewish psyche as a result of our terrible experiences. However, times have changed, and part of our unified return to core Jewish values must include parents, teachers, rabbis, and all people of influence educating and working to restore the classic Jewish approach of respecting *all* human beings and treating every person with decency and the highest levels of dignity.

≫ *Two* ≪

Racism and Discrimination

I saw such yearning in their eyes. Thousands of Ethiopian Jews were gathered in a massive courtyard to meet with me and a member of Knesset who came to see, firsthand, the desperation in Gondar. The desperation was, indeed, there. It was there as a result of their horrible poverty, but it was also there because they had not seen their closest family members in years, and in some cases, in over a decade. That's right – we have torn families apart. This was not done maliciously. Nonetheless, the reality exists: parents, children, and siblings have been brought to Israel while their children, parents, and siblings were left behind.

Despite the desperation, their eyes still expressed great yearning for Israel. They sang "*Am Yisrael Chai*" and chanted about Jerusalem while waving their official state approval for immigration with their hands. Why are these Ethiopians still there? Why are these families separated? Why isn't the Israeli government airlifting all of them to Israel to be reunited with their families and to fulfill their 2,000-year old dream to return to Israel?

There is no question that Israel demonstrated a remarkable quality when it flew over 20,000 Ethiopian Jews to Israel during Operations Moses and Solomon in 1984 and 1991. In fact, as a young yeshiva student fresh out of high school, I was privileged to welcome some of the 1991 immigrants, and to visit with them daily at the Diplomat Hotel, their first home in Israel. They were filled with such great hopes for their future. However, in reality, the Ethiopian community has struggled to acclimate to Israel. While I proudly serve in the Knesset with two Ethiopian MKs, both in my Yesh Atid party, most Ethiopian immigrants have not been given the tools necessary to advance themselves in Israel both in terms of education and in the workforce. Furthermore, those Ethiopians who miraculously navigate successfully through the challenges and obstacles of the education system and manage to earn a degree, have great difficulty finding employment. Many walk into offices and are disqualified purely because of the color of their skin. Is it possible that we have not airlifted the thousands who remain in the camp in Gondar because we fear that we cannot handle more Ethiopians who, like their predecessors, will not have the tools to succeed once they are here? Does that not border on racism and discrimination? The leaders of the Ethiopian community say this outright and we need to rally together to change this policy.

Discrimination exists in other sectors as well. Sephardic girls are routinely rejected admission to Ashkenazi-run schools. Discrimination based on the slightest differences in religious observance exists across all cultural lines. This reached its climax in Emanuel with the construction of a wall to separate slightly more observant girls from those who were slightly less observant in the very same school!

A Jewish state, which must stand for Jewish values such as

all people being created in God's image, cannot tolerate these negative developments. In *Ethics of Our Fathers*, Rabbi Eliezer teaches: "The honor of your friend should be beloved to you like your own." Rabbi Akiva teaches that "love your neighbor like yourself" is "a great rule in Torah." Finally, Hillel teaches that the message of the entire Bible can be captured in one phrase – "That which you do not want done to you, do not do to others."

There is simply no way to study these teachings and then justify racism or discrimination on any level. Such behavior is a clear violation of these tenets and must be condemned in the strongest of terms. But condemnation alone is not enough. We must push for legislation to ban all racist and discriminatory acts in Israel. Punishment for violating the law must be severe and the authorities must enforce these laws. Institutions need to be established to enable victims to lodge complaints and receive the necessary assistance to defend their rights. This would be "the Jewish way."

But the "Jewish way" has to go beyond demanding no racism or discrimination towards fellow Jews. While the issue of African "infiltrators" into Israel is no longer among the most burning in Israeli society, what happened in the spring of 2012 demonstrates a deterioration of core Jewish values. Residents of south Tel Aviv organized a rally to protest the high concentration of African migrants in their neighborhood. Knesset members participated and called on the government to detain and deport all "infiltrators." Violence was quick to break out as some members of the crowd smashed the windows of shops run by African migrants, pillaging and destroying goods. Several migrants were also physically attacked by protesters. The violence then spread to Jerusalem a few weeks later when an apartment rented by African migrants was set on fire. Injuries were sustained by four tenants and the words "get out of the neighborhood" were spray-painted on the building.

Violence towards these people runs against core Jewish values. Yes, they are "people" and deserve to be treated with dignity and respect. A quick glance through *Ethics of Our Fathers* clearly yields this point. Ben-Azzai taught "do not disgrace *any* person," without qualifying that disgracing is permitted if these people have a different skin color and you prefer not to have them in your neighborhood. Rabbi Matya taught to "greet *all* people with concern for their welfare," not with violence and heartless statements regarding the need to rid ourselves of them.

Of course, we must crack down on the criminals and there may, indeed, be legitimate grounds to deport illegal immigrants from our country. But we must adhere to core Jewish values when determining how to treat all the "infiltrators," in deciding who should and should not be expelled, and how to speak about these fellow human beings.

Is the Jewish approach to simply send these refugees back to the conditions from which they escaped without due process? Was it "the Jewish way" for a Knesset member to refer to the situation as "an 'infiltrator' enemy state has been established inside Israel?" How Jewish was the call by an MK for the IDF to shoot infiltrators who try to cross the new fence being constructed on the Egyptian border? Was a government minister reflecting any Jewish values when he bashed the "infiltrators" as a threat to Israel's character as a Jewish state, that they spread disease, and more recently, that most are involved with criminal activity? What is a greater threat to the Jewish state – infiltrators who seek asylum and refuge here or our failure to act with compassion and other fundamental Jewish values?

The Bible specifically instructs us to embrace strangers and foreigners "because we were strangers in a foreign land." As people who know what being a refugee means, we need to provide safe haven for others in need regardless of the legal classifications of their home countries. Those who do not have legitimate claims for asylum should be treated with dignity and respect by all Israelis during their detention and deportation process while those who meet the asylum criteria should be embraced and welcomed.

This notion of Jewish values must be taken one step further. We are called Jews, *Yehudim*, based on the root *hodah*, which means "thanks." We are a people who recognize the good that has been done to us by God and by others. I heard a touching presentation from one of the leaders of the Ethiopian Jewish community who related how he, his family, and thousands more crossed Sudan on their trek to be airlifted to Israel towards the end of 1984. He described how the Sudanese people built huts for them and provided them with food and water. He begged his country, Israel, to repay that favor and treat the Sudanese "infiltrators" with dignity and respect. Basic *hakarat hatov*, acknowledging the good which had been done for us by others, demands that they receive better treatment. This is the very definition of what it means to be a Jew.

The leaders of Israel, a country built by Jewish refugees and governed by Jewish, democratic values, should strive to set a more positive tone towards African migrants. We must remember that some of these asylum seekers are fleeing from the very same enemies that Israel faces today and from the same type of persecution from which Jews have fled throughout history. Public statements about the need to rid the country of a negative phenomenon, the reference to African migrants as a "threat," and the criminalization of all African migrants as "infiltrators" have increased the degree of mass hysteria.

This has fanned the flames of an already burning reality while spreading xenophobia.

Does the influx of so many non-Jews into our Jewish country create numerous challenges and obstacles? Yes, it does. However, that does not negate the fact that as people who strive to live based on core Jewish values, we all must work to bring the violence, the rhetoric, and the undignified treatment to an immediate halt.

I would like to conclude this chapter with a very practical suggestion. I had the privilege of studying for my master's degree in education at Johns Hopkins University in Baltimore, Maryland. One of the best courses I took during the program was "Multicultural Education." The purpose of the class was to prepare future educators to be successful teachers in classrooms which would include students from different backgrounds and cultures. We were taught how to be sensitive to the needs of the Hispanic, Asian, African-American, Native American, and Caribbean students who could very well end up in the same classroom in a typical United States public school. We learned about the various cultural nuances and even discovered that what could be dignified and upstanding in one culture could be an act of disrespect in another.

This course helped on the practical level of enabling teachers to properly manage their classrooms. But, the message of the class struck a much deeper chord in me and my fellow classmates. It stripped away any feelings of racism or discrimination we may have had from our upbringings. Understanding other cultures and the challenges and difficulties they faced in their past and struggle with in the present as members of a new society made us super-sensitive to their needs and bred newfound respect for all.

I recommend that Israel and all Jewish communities around

the world introduce similar programs for teachers, students, and leaders on both governmental, religious, and community levels. Once we truly understand our differences we can be sensitive to one another and respect the rights and needs of one another on the deepest of levels. This can prepare the next generation to deal with future "African infiltrator" problems, which will most certainly come our way, in a dignified and Jewish manner. And, to quote Rabbi Jacob Weinberg, my spiritual mentor, "If only we could love our fellow just as they are, this would solve all our problems."

Jews must be educated and continuously reminded of this core value of ours. We must unite to bring any semblance of racism or discrimination, both in our country and around the world, to a halt.

⇒ *Three* ⇐

Religious Coercion

MY FATHER PASSED AWAY in December 2004 and was buried in Israel. The members of the burial society, all ultra-Orthodox, treated everyone in our family with great respect. I vividly remember how they held lanterns to enable all of us to see as we walked from the chapel to the gravesite during the nighttime funeral. As we got closer to the gravesite, they politely instructed us not to go up to the actual grave. I asked why and they informed me that they were bound to the "customs of Jerusalem" which dictated that children don't participate in the actual act of burying a parent and must stand away from the grave.

I felt strongly that taking part in the actual burial was a necessary and therapeutic part of my grieving, so I pressed until they finally relented and said that whereas they cannot relax the rule for females, I, as a male, could go closer. As I reflected upon what happened at this most difficult, challenging, desperate, and emotional moment in my life, I could not stop thinking about other mourners who may not have had the courage to insist on doing what they wanted to do or even the awareness that they could do so. How many of those who wanted or needed to actively participate in the burial of a loved one were prohibited from doing so or needed to muster the emotional strength and courage to be persistent to "free" themselves to do so? I began to look into this issue some more and discovered horror stories about women who were told they could not get up in front of a crowd in order to eulogize their closest loved ones or were kept away from the gravesite against their wishes.

This type of religious coercion clearly ignores the most basic sources in our tradition. The Bible implores us to "choose" the correct path in life. This notion of "choosing" – *bechira*, in Hebrew – has been the most basic of Jewish fundamentals throughout our history. Jews have always made the choice to worship as they chose while not imposing their approach on other peoples' private lives.

Let me be clear. Throughout our history, individuals have undertaken personal stringencies and extra levels of religious observance for themselves. Many of these people were great leaders. However, they never forced their own, very personal, stringencies on others. That is actually part of why they were great leaders. Furthermore, there have always been religious people who sought to inspire fellow Jews who were less observant. But this was always based on the principle in *Ethics of Our Fathers* of "Make for yourself a rabbi" as opposed to "Force yourself on the student." If you believe that burial must be performed in a certain manner (most such customs, like keeping family members away from the grave, are based on mystical and not *halachic* reasons alone), prohibiting mourners from doing what they want to do is "forcing yourself on the student" and this kind of religious coercion is simply not the

Jewish way. The same applies to threatening arrest for women who want to wear a *tallit* at the Kotel or a multitude of other examples where what the person wants to do will have no negative impact on anyone else's personal worship. Yet, in Israel in 2013 people are being forced to conform to other individuals' perception of a custom or even the Jewish law. As Rabbi Joseph Soloveitchik explained in the late twentieth century, the term "religious coercion" is actually an oxymoron since no religious act can be coerced and maintain any religious significance for the one performing the act.

This obviously opens the door to the complicated issue of religion and state in Israel. On the one hand, the very concept of an official government rabbinate which governs lifecycle events or laws against public transportation on Shabbat seem to serve as classic examples of religious coercion. According to the sources quoted above, people should be free to choose to be religious or not without the government mixing into this issue at all. People should similarly be free to choose which rabbi and traditions they want as part of their religious services and not have these imposed on them by their government. Simply put, there should be separation of religion from state.

On the other hand, Israel is a Jewish state. What makes it a Jewish state? Is it Jewish simply because a majority of its inhabitants are Jews? Don't there have to be other defining characteristics to make it a Jewish state? Isn't this the basis for "the status quo" arrangement in which marriage, divorce, and other life cycle events are under the auspices of the Chief Rabbinate and the religion ministry?

While as an Orthodox Jew who passionately believes in the truth of my way of life, I would love to see a country where all Jews experience lifecycle events and live the way I do, I must have the intellectual honesty to say that a law which dictates that all lifecycle events in the country must be done in a religious, Orthodox manner is religious coercion.

One could argue that requiring marriages to be performed in a religious manner is not actually a religious policy but, rather, a national policy. Perhaps we need one common denominator if we want to remain a unified nation so we must take the strictest approach to marriage to insure that all marriages are accepted by everyone. The problem with that approach is that it does not work. Since laws have been passed recognizing all foreign marriages as legally binding, many Israelis travel to Cyprus or Spain to get married and then return to Israel afterwards. Those marriages, including those that are interfaith, are recognized by the Israeli government.

In addition, this attempt to preserve us as a nation is actually having the reverse effect. It is destroying us as a nation. The Talmudic principle that forcing people to do something actually pushes them away from doing it is in full force in Israel. These laws are leading hundreds of thousands of young Israelis to turn their backs on any connection to Judaism and Israel. They want no part of a country which legislates how they should experience the most important moments of their lives and desire no connection to rabbis who are making what they view as unreasonable demands, especially in the marriage process.

My party's chairman, Finance Minister MK Yair Lapid, made a remarkable observation in a presentation he made to an ultra-Orthodox audience which relates closely to the topic at hand. He pointed to the fact that the law prohibiting the public sale of leavened bread, *hametz*, on Passover is widely ignored by Israelis. The same applies to the law banning the sale of pork which some violate. However, everyone in Israel respects Yom Kippur and no one drives on that day. Why do people violate the no-bread rule on Passover and the law against selling pork, but refrain from driving on Yom Kippur? Minister Lapid suggested that the explanation is simple. There is no law prohibiting driving on Yom Kippur. It is simply a demonstration of respect. The moment there is a government law demanding religious observance, people feel coerced and have an instinct to violate it. No one wants to be forced into anything in life.

The bottom line is that in order to preserve the Jewish value which gives people free choice, to preserve Jewish unity, and to create an environment in which the masses embrace Judaism instead of detesting it, we must separate religion from politics while maintaining and even strengthening the bond between Israel as a state and Judaism. Amazingly, none other than Rabbi Eliyahu Bakshi-Doron, the former chief rabbi of Israel, has come to a similar conclusion.

Rabbi Bakshi-Doron said the following in an interview with *Techumin* magazine in 2004:

> The reality slaps us in the face. I am not aware of any person who wants to marry a non-Jew who doesn't do so because of the Marriage and Divorce law. This law may have been symbolic for the Jewish state many years ago . . . however, as one who sits on the Jewish court and is very familiar with what transpires in Israeli society, I know how much damage comes from this law . . . Non-religious Jews know how to circumvent the law and don't give the law any thought. And, sadly, this law is one of the causes for the claim of religious coercion. There is a large part of the population that simply wants to get married and they feel that this law intrudes and bothers them. And they are correct.

Rabbi Bakshi-Doron then went on to explain why from the Orthodox perspective these laws actually lead to religious problems:

> This law leads to the creation of *mamzeirut* [children defined in Jewish law as bastards]. A Jewish woman who gets married without the Orthodox ritual and laws is still a Jewish woman and her children are Jewish and part of the nation on every level. While, from the Orthodox perspective, of course, we would have preferred for them to marry in the traditional manner, it is actually worse to force her to become a married woman according to Jewish law who is then prohibited to have relationships with other men and all the problems which stem from that including her change in status.

The chief rabbi went on to state that the local religious councils must be dismantled because "they are filled with corruption and politics" and he ended the interview with the strongly worded conclusion that "government-based religious laws only lead to hatred, strife, and polarization." The core Jewish value of freedom of choice demands that we abolish laws which interfere with religious issues and this is even supported from the Orthodox perspective.

As for the desire to ensure the state's Jewish identity, many things can be done to secure that without coercion. Maintaining Shabbat as the official government day of rest certainly accomplishes that. The same goal is achieved with all government events being kosher, the Israeli army serving only kosher food, and the distribution of bibles to soldiers at IDF initiation ceremonies. We could increase the Jewish nature of the country if leaders who believe in God would actually mention God. The United States of America is the prime example in the world of separation of Church and State, but that does not stop every president from concluding speeches with the words "May God Bless America." These simple words present no threat of religious coercion, but are packed with meaning in terms of defining the country. We must do the same in Israel.

I think it necessary to establish a non-governmental Jewish Marriage Alliance which would unite Jews from all backgrounds under one umbrella organization which provides couples with an embracing, enjoyable, inspirational, and *halachically* acceptable marriage experience.

The moment we return to this core value of non-coercion, Jews will be able to embrace their country and their Judaism and we will see the most positive shifts in attitude towards Judaism emerge among Jews in Israel and throughout the world.

I conclude this chapter with a personal story which demonstrates the dangers to a free society and Jewish values if we do not put an end to the tone and environment of religious coercion which has been established in Israel from the top down.

Nearly four years ago I was enjoying a bar mitzvah celebration when my cell phone rang. I heard the shaky and scared voice of my neighbor, a friend who I knew from high school who had moved to Israel just a few months earlier. He called to tell me that he needed my help because he just received the following note in his mailbox:

> We see through the window that you have a television. If the television is not removed immediately, we are not responsible for what happens to you and your family.

I immediately ran over to his home to try to comfort him and his wife. It took a few days of investigating to find out who sent the letter, but I eventually found the group behind it and managed to secure a meeting with their "rabbi." I entered the room and saw the rabbi with menacing-looking students behind him.

I overcame my fears and attempted to engage him in dialogue. I began by pointing out that the gentile prophet Bilaam praised the Jewish people by saying "how goodly are your tents, Jacob" which the Talmud describes as a protection of privacy because the windows of their tents did not face each other. I asked him how his students could justify looking through these people's windows since this was in clear violation of the Torah's principle of privacy. He had no answer. I asked him how he and his students could force people to conform to their wishes and I then listed the Torah sources which this violated. Again, he had no answer. He asked me if I was finished reciting sources and then he began a monologue about their history. He explained that coercion and violence is how they have learned to deal with the "Zionist invasion of Israel."

Despite the lack of dialogue, I managed to convince the "rabbi" and his followers that it was in their own best interests to rescind the television threat. They ultimately did. But this experience opened my eyes to the dangers when religious coercion goes unchecked. Such an environment fosters a mentality which empowers extremist groups to coerce everyone in Israel to conform to their specific understanding of Judaism. This "rabbi" and his followers made it clear that they viewed the secular and religious Zionist communities as the cause for all problems, illness, and tragedies in Israeli society. They also stated that they believe that it is permissible to use all means at their disposal to rid their neighborhoods and ultimately the country of the lifestyles which they see as "contaminating" and "defiling" the Land of Israel. And sure enough, four years later, in the fall of 2011, I was reintroduced to some of those same fanatics on the streets of Bet Shemesh as they unleashed their horrifying verbal assaults on seven-year old Naama Margolese and her elementary schoolmates as they simply tried to walk home from the Orot girls' school.

These violent fundamentalists are the extreme. The average and mainstream ultra-Orthodox Jew would never think of coercing, threatening, or being violent. But extremism of this kind doesn't emerge out of a vacuum. It begins with unnecessary stringencies imposed by rabbinic leaders, and continues to government level coercion, which by nature spreads and becomes even more prevalent and extreme. I believe that Jewish organizations and individual voters must bolster and support courageous leaders and parties who seek to take on the establishment and separate religious services from the government. Furthermore, laws must be in place to protect citizens from coercion within communities and institutions. And finally, we must reintroduce an environment which embraces all Jews and encourages religious services with sincere care and love.

The time has come for Jews from all backgrounds to work together to demand an end to coercion on all levels and to return to a Judaism in which every human being is free to exercise their most basic right while not causing harm to others – choice. This approach will enable us to take giant steps towards a united Jewish people.

⇒ *Four* ⇐

Women

IT STARTED WITH SIGNS in certain areas dictating how women should dress:

> To women and girls who pass through our neighborhood: We beg you with all our hearts. PLEASE NO NOT PASS THROUGH OUR NEIGHBORHOOD IN IMMODEST CLOTHES. Modest clothes include: closed blouses with long sleeves, long skirts – no trousers, no tight-fitting clothes.

Then women were asked to ride in the back of certain buses. This problem became so serious that the Supreme Court had to order buses to post the following signs:

> Passengers may sit wherever they choose. Bothering passengers about this may be considered a criminal offense.

Next, women who went walking, jogging, or biking were screamed at, spat upon, and even had rocks thrown at them. As one woman described:

> I was towards the end of my usual bike ride when I suddenly heard something hit my wheel. And, then, another noise. I

looked to the side and there was a guy throwing rocks in my direction. Luckily he had bad aim or I could have been hurt badly. I was scared for my life.

Then the leaders of my hometown, Bet Shemesh, began defining the city as "ultra-Orthodox" despite a non-ultra-Orthodox majority and began routinely removing women from public signs and advertisements. When the municipality published a booklet about all the city activities there were no pictures of any females. When confronted regarding the fact that no women or girls appeared in any of the pictures, the city spokesman explained:

> The booklet was published for the entire city and we needed to take into account those populations which would find pictures of women or girls to be offensive.

The mistreatment of females in Bet Shemesh reached the lowest of lows when grown men blocked sidewalks to protest the "immodesty" of young elementary school girls, screaming at them:

> Leave our neighborhood! Stop defiling our neighborhood! *Prutza*! [literally, "immodest one" with the connotation of "prostitute"]

While the girls were spared any serious physical assaults, Natalie Moshiach and Vered Daniel, both non-religious but quite traditional, were not as fortunate. Each one made the mistake of simply appearing in an extremist neighborhood. Natalie's car was stoned while she sat inside and Vered's car was stoned as she was taking her baby out to buy a stroller in a baby shop. The righteous and courageous ultra-Orthodox women who own the store shielded her until it was safe for her to leave.

At a recent meeting of the two, Natalie said: "I prepared myself to die right there." Vered confirmed feeling the same.

None of these are hearsay or rumors. These horrors occurred right around the corner from my home in 2012. It started with the acceptance of signs dictating how women should dress and has reached the point of stoning.

As I, along with other political and religious leaders, always point out, the number of religious Jews who act in the manners described above is relatively small. It must be made clear that the overwhelming majority of Jews, including ultra-Orthodox, would never intentionally harm anyone. However, there was and continues to be a passive acceptance of this behavior and an unwillingness to act against these extremists by the Israeli government and authorities, from Jewish leaders, and the broader Jewish family. This can only be classified as disrespect of women and girls. If one truly believes in equality and absolute respect for women and their welfare then one cannot justify remaining silent in the face of these attacks, even if doing so exposes us to risks and threats from these violent extremists.

But, aside from the silence, our country has accepted certain policies which feed this disrespect for women. My wife and I chose to bring our daughter to the Kotel, the Western Wall, on the night she turned 12. We figured there could be no better way to begin her life as a bat mitzvah than praying at the site where our ancient Temple stood. I prepared myself for inspiration as I watched her approach the wall with her mother. Instead, however, I experienced great indignation. The men's side of the partition consisted of a single line of men, with gaps along the entire length of the wall. The women's side, which is far less than half the size of the men's side, was jammed with women six rows deep. My wife could only bring my daughter up to the wall after waiting a long time and, even then, had to respectfully push her way through. I watched this happen and could not believe the disgrace to my daughter, to my wife, and to all women. Then, as I continued to observe my daughter praying, I noticed how other women had to wait and push to get close to the wall while on the men's side, they could easily and immediately approach the wall.

Equality for women is something that needs to be addressed in the clearest of terms. Once we allow this subtle mistreatment of women at the Kotel or posted signs instructing women how to dress in detail, the road has been paved for verbal assault against young girls and stonings of adult women by extremists. And, aside from the fear of the emerging violent extremism, equality for women is plainly and simply what Jewish values demand.

The beginning of the Bible describes the creation of the first human being with the words, "male and female He created *them*." If there was only one being, why does it describe it as "male and female" and as "them?" The Talmud explains that the original being embodied both male and female character-istics and was subsequently separated into two beings. Why weren't they created as separate male and female beings from the outset?

We turn to Rabbi Samson Raphael Hirsch who explains:

> So that what was previously one creature was now two, and thereby the complete equality of women forever attested.

Complete equality! Not a secondary being who can be told to go to the back of the bus or who can be removed from all pictures.

But our tradition goes even beyond demanding equality and actually places women on a pedestal. The Talmud teaches that the Jews were redeemed from slavery in Egypt due to

the merit of Jewish women, that women did not worship the
golden calf and they declined to accept the negative report of
the spies about the Land of Israel. Our tradition teaches that
the salvations of both the Hanukah and Purim stories occurred
because our women rose to the occasion. In Jewish thought,
women have *binah yeteira* – an advanced ability to understand
and comprehend, an attribute which has saved the Jewish
people numerous times throughout history. Finally, Maimonides, the Spanish philosopher, taught in medieval times, when
most men in the world treated women as nothing more than
property, that "a husband must honor his wife more than his
own self."

The most basic erosion of equality, instructing women to
ride in the back of a bus, has also been addressed in previous
generations. Rabbi Moshe Feinstein, the great authority on
Jewish law in the Orthodox world in the twentieth century,
made this very clear in his responsa where he ruled that there
was no problem with riding the New York City subway during
rush hour. This response applies all the more so when men and
women are simply sitting in close proximity on a bus.

Aside from the fact that Jewish law certainly permits men
and women to sit together on the bus or walk on the same side
of the street, there is actually a specific transgression that oc-
curs when extreme actions are taken to force gender separation.
Judaism clearly states that not embarrassing others is one of
its primary tenets, and that is the exact transgression which
transpires when men harass and intimidate women for sitting
in the front part of the bus or put up signs demanding that
women dress in a certain manner. In certain circumstances,
Jewish law actually permits one to transgress a prohibition if
doing so will preserve and protect the dignity of a fellow human being. Therefore, even according to a person's skewed

understanding that Jewish law does mandate the separation of men and women in these circumstances, there would certainly be no justification for demeaning a woman by forcing her to move to the back of the bus. Granted, there are traditional laws which mandate the separation of men and women during prayer and other very specific times, but nothing beyond that. The Bible opens the door for women to be full members of society and cautions that it is the *man's* responsibility not to "stray after your eyes." Men can be easily tempted and they have the obligation to control those temptations.

Rabbi Shlomo Zalman Auerbach, one of the great Israeli ultra-Orthodox leaders in the late twentieth century, used to ride a public bus every day to yeshiva. One day, one of his students saw the rabbi get off the bus at a stop nowhere near the yeshiva. When Rabbi Auerbach arrived at the yeshiva a bit later, the student asked him why he got off the bus at the wrong stop. Rabbi Auerbach explained:

> I have no problem riding the bus with women, and women often sit down next to me. Today, a woman who was dressed very provocatively sat down next to me. I would never embarrass her by commenting about her dress or moving away from her. I waited a few stops and then pretended like I reached my destination and simply got off and waited for the next bus.

This was a wise rabbi, a great person, and true leader who understood core Jewish values.

There is no question that the first step in addressing the horrible, violent extremist treatment of women described at the beginning of this chapter is to combat all hints of religious extremism and denigration of women. The second and more fundamental step is to end institutionalized disrespect of women. So, at the Kotel for example, the partition should be placed down the middle of the plaza or a portable partition could be put into the middle of the Kotel plaza, to allow for some flexibility, at least during the hours in which the women's side is most crowded. That is equality! That is respect! The partition can be shifted based on the agreed upon needs of either side. The third step is much broader and not any less important. We must strive to put Jewish women in leadership positions and we must have zero tolerance for discrimination of women in any form.

The Bible is quite remarkable with regards to the role of Jewish women during historical eras when women had no place in the public sphere. Miriam, sister of Moses and Aaron, was a clear leader. Devora served as the judge of the entire nation, Hulda was an important advisor to King Josiah, and Atalya was queen of the Judean Kingdom, just to cite several examples. Bruriah was accepted as a scholar who participated in public debates about Jewish law during the Talmudic period.

The current Knesset reflects a very positive change in this area and I am so proud to serve in the Yesh Atid party alongside eight female MKs (out of 19!). But women still hold only 34% of government leadership jobs such as director-general positions and other primary administrative roles in government offices and institutions. Placing women in leadership positions will increase their general standing in society and will also insure that focus is placed on caring for women's needs.

Our women are certainly capable of achieving the highest of positions. A 2010 report indicated that 60.2% of females in Israel qualify for their matriculation certificates in contrast to 49.4% of males. Furthermore, 55% of those enrolled in Israeli undergraduate programs are women. But the successes stop there. When it comes to the workforce, approximately half can only find work in low-paying positions such as secretaries, house cleaners, kitchen staff, etc. Women's average monthly salaries are only 64% of average male salaries. In 2005–2006 more than ⅕ of women were categorized as "impoverished."

Jewish values require that we work to restore the equality established at the beginning of the Bible by elevating more women to positions of power, legislating complete equality with regard to hiring practices, and enforcing punitive measures against any groups that denigrate women for religious purposes.

I stood on the streets of Bet Shemesh, attempting to protect school girls from the verbal and physical assaults of religious extremists. These thugs had hatred and animosity in their eyes. A societal demonization of the female gender was reflected in these episodes.

From my perspective, having seen the extremism firsthand, the silence of the masses reflects the erosion, or even the collapse, of our value system and priorities. It is time to reorder those priorities to ensure that no woman or girl has to experience anything of this sort again and to ensure that my younger daughters and future granddaughters will not need to struggle while approaching the Kotel and will be free to go wherever they want, whenever they want. When women feel completely embraced and accepted throughout the Jewish world, we will have taken a huge step towards the goal of complete unity around core Jewish values.

Five

Accepting All Jews as Jews

DANIELLE GOSSMAN-VITORY has a Jewish mother and gentile father. According to every opinion in the spectrum of classic Jewish sources, she is Jewish. Danielle, who was raised Reform, went on a Birthright program to Israel during her first year of college and then studied in an Orthodox seminary during her second visit. She started to become more observant and when she returned to San Diego, her hometown, she accepted an invitation to Shabbat dinner with friends. Rafi, an electrical engineer from Israel who was in California to gain professional experience, was at the Shabbat dinner and the two fell in love. After completing her degree, Danielle returned to Israel and she and Rafi got engaged.

Preparing for her marriage, what she thought would be a wonderful process, became a torturous series of demands from the Israeli rabbinate to prove that she was, in fact, Jewish. The letter from her Chabad rabbi in college was not enough. Her parents were married in a Reform synagogue and therefore there was no valid *ketuva* (marriage contract) from their wedding. She was asked to produce her grandparents' marriage certificate but could not find it. A photograph of her grand-mother's grave in a Jewish cemetery was rejected as proof. The rabbinate finally accepted her uncle's valid *ketuva* from his marriage in a Conservative synagogue, together with his birth certificate and her mother's birth certificate (to prove that they were brother and sister and both had the same Jewish mother), along with Danielle's birth certificate. Danielle had to have all these documents certified by a notary and translated into He-brew which cost her 200 shekel per page. She received formal approval two weeks before the wedding date.

Quite surprisingly, the rabbinate issued her an apology for all the trouble. They told her, "We thought you were Russian!"

This specific story has a happy ending. Danielle and Rafi are married and officially recognized as such by the State. They live in Ra'anana, and Danielle is completely accepted by Rafi's family. But think about the number of Jews who have been turned away by this lack of acceptance and who are no longer interested in being part of our nation. Travelling throughout Israel and the world, I have heard dozens of horror stories about people who are Jews, yet still had to jump through hoops to prove it – either for the right to immigrate to Israel or in order to get married in Israel. Many have decided to remain in the Diaspora because they do not want to live in a country that rejected their Jewishness, and many don't want their children to have to deal with these same issues in the future.

The part of Danielle's story which stung me the most was the apology with the explanation that "we thought you were Russian." I had the great honor of spending time in Tbilisi, Georgia, soon after the fall of the former Soviet Union. I bonded with Jewish children who demonstrated a real thirst for knowledge and connection to their spiritual heritage. Their love for the Sabbath and desire to hear about Israel inspired me to be more appreciative of the Sabbath and to be even more Zionistic. Their pride in being Jewish reawakened my Jewish pride. The mere thought of these special, young Jews emerging from the Iron Curtain to arrive in an Israel where they would have to overcome hurdles and obstacles to prove their Judaism should embarrass and infuriate Jews worldwide.

In light of Danielle's story and the tens of thousands of Jews from around the world who have been made to feel "less Jewish" or even "not Jewish" by the State of Israel, the time has come for Jews from all backgrounds around the world to unite and declare, "A Jew is a Jew regardless of the level of religious observance, lifestyle, or affiliation. We embrace all fellow Jews as members of our family, and will never reject a fellow Jew for any reason."

A story regarding a well-known Orthodox rabbi, Rabbi Aryeh Levin, demonstrates the approach which Jews should have towards one another. Rabbi Levin was walking in his hometown, Jerusalem, when he noticed a young soldier he recognized who was home on break from his military service.

"Hello," said Rabbi Levin who was already an older man. "Please come to my home and share some tea with me. I would like to hear about what you are doing."

The young soldier seemed uncomfortable and replied, "I don't think it's right for me to come visit you. I don't even wear a *kippah* anymore."

Rabbi Levin, wearing his black hat and long black coat, took the soldier's hand into his own and with a smile on his face he said: "Don't you see? I'm very short. I cannot look above your head to see whether you are wearing a *kippah* or not. However, I can see your heart and your heart is big and kind, and that's what counts." Rabbi Levin then paused and added, "You are also a soldier placing your life at risk for all of us in Israel.

Please drink tea with me – your '*kippah*' is probably bigger than mine."

A Jew is a Jew. Our numbers are very small. We need each other's support, respect, and love. Nothing else is acceptable and the State of Israel, as the Jewish homeland, must accept and embrace all Jews as Jews. No value can be more basic and unifying.

The situation becomes more complicated with regard to people who opt to join the Jewish people. We live in a world where so many people around the world want to be Jews, have made personal sacrifices to be Jews, and are not accepted as Jews. The conversion crisis is not a simple one to solve. After all, as opposed to the topic being discussed until this point in the chapter – the imperative to accept people who are Jewish as Jews – we now turn to people who are not Jewish but want to convert where the issue of Jewish law comes into the picture.

I believe this issue must be divided into different categories. The first and most pressing relates to non-Jewish Russian immigrants in Israel who have a Jewish father or grandfather but not a Jewish mother and are therefore not Jewish according to Jewish law. They serve in the Israeli army, study in Israeli universities, speak Hebrew, carry Jewish names, and of course, meet other Jews. A high percentage of them seek to convert to Judaism, but have been faced with resistance by the rabbinate which questions their level of commitment to religious observance, a prerequisite for conversion. I believe we should implement the teachings in the book, *Zera Yisrael*, by former MK Rabbi Haim Amsalem. The approach, coming from an ultra-Orthodox perspective, dictates that according to traditional Jewish law we not only *can* convert these immigrants, but we also *must* convert them. We, as Jews, cannot tolerate a situation in which people who were physically persecuted in the former Soviet Union for being Jews are now suffering socially and religiously in Israel because they are non-Jews.

Jewish tradition demands that we not relate to these Russian immigrants of Jewish descent as gentiles. While they are not Jewish, they actually fall into a unique category called *zera Yisrael* ("descendants of Israel"). Rabbi Tzadok Rabinowitz, a well-respected nineteenth century biblical scholar from Lublin, Poland explained that Isaiah referred to *zera Yisrael* when he described the "lost ones" who would return to become part of the Jewish people upon our return to our homeland.

Regarding the criteria for conversion, the Talmud clearly requires that we must only teach the conversion candidate "some lenient and some strict commandments." Furthermore, both Maimonides and Rabbi Joseph Karo, author of the *Shulchan Aruch*, the Code of Jewish Law, teach that if a conversion transpired accidentally with absolutely no discussion regarding the convert's mitzvah acceptance, the conversion remains valid and the convert is a full-fledged Jew. This does not mean that we should not require an acceptance of *mitzvot*. However, it certainly downgrades the overall severity and stringency with which many view this step in the process. Some traditional sources are clear that we can be lenient when it comes to *zera Yisrael* who want to convert and accept them with a commitment to some basic traditions.

The candidates in question accept to fast on Yom Kippur, to refrain from eating leavened bread on Passover, agree to recite the *Kiddush* prayer and light the candles on Sabbath eve, and those in the IDF risk their lives to protect the Jewish state (what greater mitzvah can there be?). We have enough classic texts and sources to serve as a basis to permit the conversions of these *zera Yisrael* immigrants. In fact, we should be keenly motivated to convert them, especially in light of their desire and intention to observe these fundamental commandments.

One additional scenario demands that we convert these immigrants immediately on the basis of the rabbinic opinions and statements quoted above. If we don't allow them to convert, these immigrants are going to marry our children anyway. They grow up together, go through elementary and high school together, serve in the army together, and study in university together. When this happens, within the next few decades, Israel will be ripped apart with disputes regarding which citizens are Jews and which are not. Non-Jewish children will be raised as Jews, but will not be recognized as Jews by the rabbinate or the state. This will polarize Israel in ways it has never been polarized before. True concern for the future of Judaism and the Jewish people requires us to anticipate future challenges and problems and address them now. In our current circumstance that means relying on those valid and lenient opinions to convert these immigrants to Judaism. They are our extended family who, through no fault of their own, were forced away from the fold. They now live in Israel and want to return. We should embrace them.

The issue becomes far more complicated when we shift to conversions of gentiles who don't come from Jewish descent, but I believe that if we are living by core Jewish values, we should begin the process of exploring ways for all Jews to work together on that front as well. Doing so does not mean we agree about theology and is not an endorsement of one movement or another. Rather, this reflects membership in the same family trying to find a way to get along and make progress despite strong differences of opinion.

Various attempts have been made to try to create a unifying

conversion policy for all Jews. In the 1950s, Rabbi Joseph Soloveitchik attempted to negotiate the formation of a national religious court whose objective was to oversee conversions and create unified standards for marriage and divorce. The agreement included a clause stating that the religious judges who oversaw the actual conversion would be Orthodox. However, the attempt failed and many who were involved said that the failure came from authorities on the Orthodox side who felt that any kind of cooperation with the Conservative leadership was forbidden.

Another attempt at unity was organized and actually implemented in Denver, Colorado in the late 1970s. A joint Orthodox, Traditional, Conservative, and Reform *Bet Din* was formed to promote uniform standards for conversion to Judaism. Over a five-year period they performed some 750 conversions. The agreement worked as follows: Rabbis began the initial process of instructing potential converts. Candidates then enrolled in a course about the fundamentals of Judaism run and taught by rabbis from all denominations. Participants would agree to basic Jewish observances like fasting on Yom Kippur, joining a synagogue, lighting candles on Shabbat and holidays, and would be informed about dietary laws and "keeping a Jewish household." Then a panel of rabbis representing different movements, always including an Orthodox representative, examined the candidate. If the candidate was approved by all, then three Orthodox rabbis formed the religious court necessary to approve each conversion and oversaw the last steps of immersion in the ritual bath and ritual circumcision for men.

However, in 1983 the joint *Bet Din* was dissolved due to two issues. One was the decision of the Reform movement to change the definition of Jewishness to include patrilineal descent. The second was significant opposition to the initiative from the mainstream Orthodox rabbinate which viewed the Orthodox rabbis involved in this initiative as fringe and rogue.

In 1989 and 1990, Israeli Prime Minister Yitzhak Shamir led an effort to find a solution to what became known as the "Who is a Jew?" problem. Cabinet Secretary Elyakim Rubenstein negotiated secretly with rabbis from all streams. They developed a plan to create a joint panel that would interview conversion candidates. There would be dialogue among all streams throughout the process, but an Orthodox rabbinic court would oversee the actual conversion. Reform leaders were unhappy with the requirement that the religious court be Orthodox, but they ultimately agreed. The plan was dismantled when more extreme Orthodox leadership got word of it. Rabbi Norman Lamm, president of Yeshiva University, remarked that had this unified conversion plan not been torpedoed, he had hoped to extend this program to the area of divorces as well, to confront the problem of "bastard children" which arises when divorces are not conducted according to traditional Jewish law.

In 1997, Prime Minister Netanyahu appointed the Ne'eman Commission, headed by Yaakov Ne'eman, an Orthodox Jew, to focus specifically on the issue of Russian immigrants, and to address the broader "Who is a Jew?" question as well. The committee recommended the creation of rabbinic panels with representation from all three movements to prepare potential candidates for conversion. The actual conversion, itself, would remain under the domain of the Orthodox rabbinate. Does this formula sound familiar? The plan was rejected by the Israeli chief rabbinate in 1998.

I am well aware of the complexity of the issues at hand and the fears of converting those who do not qualify for conversion. Furthermore, I recognize the fact that it will be difficult to find a solution which works according to traditional Jewish law.

However, I do think it is time for a shift in attitude. Polarization among Jews is at an all-time high, right along with assimilation and intermarriage. Let's begin the process by recognizing all Jews as Jews. Perhaps that will break down some barriers and enable dialogue. This will foster cooperation, allow us to work together on the issues, and ultimately formulate legislation we all agree to. A next step could be partnering to solve the conversion crisis in Israel and implementing more moderate policies for *zera Yisrael* which conform to Orthodox tradition. Once that has been solved perhaps we can begin to explore a broader, unified conversion policy. The Orthodox side would not have to give up on "*halacha*" but would be "compromising" in terms of both a willingness to work together with other groups and finding leniencies within "*halacha*" where possible. The other streams would need to recognize that not every conversion sought would be approved.

If we truly believe that "all Jews are responsible for one another," and reflect on both our unified histories and the number of modern-day enemies who see us all as one unit which they seek to eliminate, can we afford to do any less than at least try to find some common ground and create unity in these areas? Our efforts may fail, but we have no hope if we don't make the attempt. Moreover, based on what I, myself, have witnessed and heard about the degree of distance and outright animosity among Jews, I suggest that in the very act of trying to find some common ground we are reaffirming our peoplehood.

Restoring the embracing conversion policies of old will take time and significant effort on a rabbinic and political level. I certainly encourage leaders to take these steps, and for voters, students, and congregants to pressure their leaders to address these issues. This is certainly a major focus of mine in the Knesset. But, embracing all Jews is something all individuals can take upon themselves from this moment onward. If we all do, this no doubt will have influence on the rabbinic and political leadership in Israel as well, and we can all unite and live our lives under the guiding principle that "your '*kippah*' is probably bigger than mine."

⇒ *Six* ⇐

The Workforce

I HAD THE INCREDIBLE PRIVILEGE to study in an outstanding institution, Ner Israel Rabbinical College in Baltimore, Maryland. It is a yeshiva in every sense of the word and produces Torah scholars of the highest caliber. Many of the top rabbinic leaders, educators, and authors in the Jewish world come from the ranks of Ner Israel. And now for the surprise: Most Ner Israel students attend university alongside their Torah studies. While in recent decades a philosophy of Torah study alone with absolutely no preparation or training for earning a livelihood has emerged in the ultra-Orthodox world, the Ner Israel approach represents the authentic Jewish outlook. Restoring this approach throughout the Jewish world will open all Jews to being part of broader society and will combat the isolationism which breeds much of the religious extremism and leads to polarization.

Traditional Jewish sources clearly teach that learning a trade in order to support one's family with dignity, alongside religious studies and living a Jewish lifestyle, is the highest of ideals. For example, the Jerusalem Talmud interprets the Torah's instruction to "choose life" as a command to engage in a trade. The Babylonian Talmud teaches that "a father must teach his son a trade. Anyone who does not teach his son a trade is as if he taught his son robbery." Our tradition also instructs: "Acquire for yourself a trade together with Torah." The Babylonian Talmud goes as far as saying that "a person who earns a living from his own handiwork is greater than one who fears Heaven." *Ethics of Our Fathers* states emphatically that "any Torah not accompanied by work will end up being nullified and will lead to sin." And, finally, the famed thirteenth century French codifier of Jewish law, Moshe ben Yaakov (the "Smag"), actually uses the biblical words "six days you should work" as a biblical commandment that people must go to work during the week and support their families.

A glance through the Talmud reveals that along with being great Torah scholars, the spiritual leaders of earlier generations earned their living as doctors, tailors, launderers, farmers, carpenters, land surveyors, shoemakers and repairmen, woodchoppers, beer makers, bakers, smiths, trap makers, engravers, skin-tanners, mill workers, scribes, ditch diggers, bundle and beam transporters, wool merchants, and weavers.

All the above sources no doubt served as the basis for the following teaching from Maimonides, himself an esteemed Torah scholar and world-class physician (*Laws of Torah Study* 3:10–11):

> Any person who makes the decision to study Torah without a livelihood and to sustain himself from charity – such a person desecrates God, disgraces Torah, extinguishes the light of religion, does himself ill, and removes himself from the World to Come . . . and our sages also commanded that a person should not earn a living from Torah. . . . It is a high level for a person to earn a living from his own toil, and a trait of the

saintly. Through this, a person earns all the honor and good in this world and the next.

This approach continued until more modern times. For example, the fifteenth century ethical work, *Orchot Tzadikim,* teaches that:

> A person must find middle ground with two responsibilities and set aside hours for Torah study and for work in this world, and must strengthen himself to do both . . . neither should take away from the other.

The famed Rabbi Judah Loew of sixteenth-century Prague relates in his book, *Netivot Olam,* which focuses on man's obligations of conduct:

> When a person is busy with two pursuits – work to provide for what his body needs, and Torah for completion of his soul – he will not find any sin.

So, it is clear that Jewish tradition advocates learning a trade and that this is not a contradiction to intensive Torah study. In order to prepare all Jewish children for a future trade, we must teach them the most basic of "secular" studies such as language, math, and science. Programs to enable continued Torah studies along with earning a university degree are not only consistent with our tradition, but are also a necessity according to our heritage. The Ner Israel model proves that this is possible and does not in any way take away from progress on the Torah scholarship side of the equation.

We must also remember that most young men are not capable of full-time study for their entire lives but tens of thousands are trapped in a system which demands this of them. What do we do about the children of the mother from Bnei Brak who called me and said she is going to lose seven of her sons who are not cut out to study Torah all day, but are not being taught that they can balance Torah study with other pursuits? What about the group of 18- and 19-year-olds who met me in a park in Givat Shmuel at 1:00 a.m. who want to remain ultra-Orthodox and study Torah while pursuing their dreams of becoming doctors and engineers? I believe that the time has come for us to focus on the needs of those children and young men and enable them to be true to themselves and our traditions rather than this new approach which essentially forces all ultra-Orthodox young men into full-time Torah learning.

Maimonides, at the end of the *Laws of the Sabbatical and Jubilee Years*, does elaborate on the benefits of doing nothing but studying Torah. Chaim ibn Attar, one of the greatest biblical commentators of the early eighteenth century, explains that this teaching refers to a situation in which people choose to support full-time Torah scholars in partnerships. Maimonides, in the *Laws of Torah Study* previously quoted, is referring to a person who places a burden on the nation through his learning, essentially forcing others to support him. Someone who loves Torah study and forges a private arrangement which enables him to study Torah while receiving the support of a private individual is truly blessed. I enjoy studying Torah and can understand that people who don't feel the pull to do anything else could enjoy learning Torah all day throughout their lives. However, as Maimonides states, no person can choose to place the burden of supporting himself on the community. We must unite to ensure that this practice ceases and thus alleviate a tremendous burden that has been placed on shoulders of the entire Jewish community and bring an end to this source of disunity.

A clarification is in order regarding this "burden" which is being borne by the community. In Israel, more than 50 percent

of the ultra-Orthodox community lives below the poverty line.
Those living in poverty rely on public and private funds to feed
their families. It must be noted that employment rates among
the ultra-Orthodox in Israel are improving and are now over
40%. However, the problem of poverty and dependence on
funding sources also extends to the employed ultra-Orthodox
due to the lack of general education and preparation at younger
ages for entry into the workforce. This leads to 66% of ultra-Orthodox women and 45% of the men who enter the workforce
finding work in community jobs, education, health or public
service fields. Only 38% of the ultra-Orthodox possess some
computer know-how, and only 2.3% of the ultra-Orthodox
who have joined the work force enter the commercial markets.

In short, the focus on exclusive Torah study, the negative
perspective on entering the workforce, and the lack of general education in the ultra-Orthodox community do create a
burden on the broader community and do not represent the
Jewish way according to Maimonides.

Having said all of the above, I must make mention of what
I see as our communal responsibility to produce and support
elite Torah scholars. It has always been part of our tradition to
identify a select group of young men who have the potential
and drive needed to spend their entire lives studying Torah
and become our future Torah giants – *Gedolei Torah*. We, as a
community, should not only support this small group of scholars, but should also feel blessed to have that opportunity. The
number of exceptional Torah scholars in each generation who
fit these criteria is quite small, but, even today, we must find
those elite scholars and support them. One of the arguments
against secular studies and joining the workforce is that the
only way to maintain quality Torah scholarship is to focus exclusively on Torah. First of all, let us be clear that the number

of Torah scholars produced by Ner Israel, despite the fact that its students attend secular universities, is astounding. The best and the brightest of Ner Israel can hold their own with the Torah scholars of the Israeli ultra-Orthodox community. The same applies to institutions such as Landers and Yeshiva University, centers of Torah scholarship that provide college classes on their own campuses.

Second, providing the non-elite students with pursuits other than Torah study will actually strengthen their Torah study. It is time for the ultra-Orthodox world to admit and confront the reality that most boys are not capable of studying all day and night. Expecting the average boy to do so is unrealistic. Providing them with some general studies and recreation will enable them to learn better during their Torah study hours. Freeing them to train for a career will actually lead to more dedication and focus in their Torah study. Without a doubt, earning a dignified livelihood will provide young married men with the peace of mind to join tens of thousands, throughout the country and the world, in focusing intently on their Torah study during their non-working hours. The quality of their study will actually increase because they are taking time to work. I have many friends who are attorneys, accountants, doctors, and businessmen who have completed the study of the Talmud numerous times. They know it well, have authored Torah books of their own, and teach Torah classes in their spare time.

Since I have become identified with the battle against religious extremism, ultra-Orthodox Jews from throughout Israel have reached out to me. They beg me and others to continue in our efforts to free them from poverty into which they have been forced. They understand that Judaism embraces earning a dignified living and learning general studies. They have also revealed something else to me. Young men who do "break" from the mold and go to work suddenly realize that the outside world is not the devil. They come to know and appreciate the goodness that exists among secular and more modern religious Jews. They begin to understand that we can have strong ideological disagreements, but still get along and even work together. This empowers them to depart from the extremism and fanaticism within their communities while continuing to live a strict, religious lifestyle. The "us" against "them" attitude which has been preached to them from the youngest of ages comes crumbling down and a willingness to live in harmony with respect for one another emerges. Secular Israelis also begin to respect the values of the ultra-Orthodox community as they begin to work together with them in the labor market. Hatreds which they have harbored towards the ultra-Orthodox disappear. Doing whatever we can to help the ultra-Orthodox enter the workforce both in Israel and around the world may be the most significant step we can take in re-establishing feelings of tolerance and unity among all Jews.

Secular-run companies throughout Israel must display openness and unity by opening doors to ultra-Orthodox employment while rabbinic and political leaders must have the courage to stand up and change a culture which promotes isolationism and dependency. For thousands of years, every Jewish husband has accepted the following declaration in his marriage contract:

> Be my wife according to the practice of Moses and Israel, and I will cherish, honor, support, and maintain you in accordance with the custom of Jewish husbands who cherish, honor, support, and maintain their wives faithfully . . . according to the law of Moses and Israel; and I will also give you your food, clothing, and necessities. . . .

What more needs to be said?

Seven

Sharing National Responsibilities

As a child growing up right outside Washington, DC, I often participated in demonstrations outside the Soviet Embassy. We chanted "one, two, three, four, open up the iron door, five, six, seven, eight, let our people emigrate" and sang "*Am Yisrael Chai*." As a young child, I did not understand how our efforts could possibly help people like Yosef Mendelovich and Anatoly Sharansky whose faces I knew only from pictures on our signs. But now, thirty years later, I have had the honor of meeting these heroes in Israel and hearing them explain how much our protests meant to their cause. Natan Sharansky related the following:

> I was languishing in prison with Russian and Ukrainian nationals, and they told me that I was going to be freed at some point. I asked why they were so convinced about this and they responded, "Because your people are out in the streets all over the world demanding your release. No one has even taken notice of us."

The Talmudic teaching, "all Jews are responsible for one

another" is not just meant to be a nice, feel-good saying. It is meant in its literal sense. Jews throughout the ages, from Abraham, who risked his life to save his nephew, Lot, to the heroic decision-makers and soldiers of the Entebbe rescue mission, have put this value into practice.

We live in a time when leaders of communities are using their Judaism as a reason not to serve in the Israeli army. They claim to be doing so in consonance with our tradition. The Bible is the most obvious reference text for a Jew who is unsure of how to act. There can be no clearer source regarding how we should behave than when the Bible sends a clear message which cannot be misconstrued or interpreted in ways to suit people's personal agendas. The issue of Jews not serving in the IDF or sharing in the nation's other burdens is addressed directly by the Bible. Towards the end of *Numbers*, the fourth book of the Bible, two tribes asked Moses to permit them to dwell on the eastern side of the Jordan River. They preferred the quality of life there to what awaited them in Israel proper. Moses responded with a rebuke: "Shall your brothers go out to battle while you settle here?" Moses then grants their request, but only if they first join the Jewish army in their fight for the Land of Israel. Any question regarding whether citizens can simply opt out of army service because they choose to have other priorities should never even arise. Moses made that clear.

Truth be told, we should not even have to resort to Moses's rebuke to resolve this issue. Jewish tradition is replete with teachings regarding the responsibility we have towards one another. How can anyone study the teachings such as "love your neighbor like yourself," "do not stand idly by over the blood of your brother," and the above quoted "all Jews are responsible for one another," without internalizing that Judaism demands sharing the national responsibilities?

This call for all citizens to serve in the IDF applies to secular objectors as well. However, as an Orthodox rabbi, I choose to focus on religious objectors who use religious grounds to question the assertion that all Israelis should serve. After all, they argue, doesn't the army present moral and spiritual challenges and obstacles for the soldiers? The answer to this question is very straightforward. To begin with, religious soldiers have been serving since the State was founded and have always been served kosher food and were able to pray and have their religious needs met. The IDF has made further adjustments in recent years, creating special frameworks to suit soldiers of all religious backgrounds. Nahal Haredi, a unit made up of religious soldiers offers daily Torah classes and prayer services and all spiritual sensitivities are taken into account. The Shahar program is offered to Haredi men who have already learned Torah for four or more years after the age of 18. This program offers twenty-six different vocational tracks including computer programming, electrical engineering, technical writing, and even truck-driving. These soldiers are given off on Friday, Shabbat, and all holidays and all their religious needs, including *kashrut* and those which are gender-related are met.

There will always be new challenges for an army with both religious and non-religious soldiers. The army brass is prepared to address those challenges in consultation with ultra-Orthodox leaders to make sure that all soldiers feel comfortable in the IDF without it being a threat to their way of life. Based on all of the above, in the eyes of anyone looking at the situation objectively, the suggestion that any group cannot perform Israeli army service because of religious concerns must be put to rest.

Of course, as in any military, exemptions are granted for various reasons. However, the teachings of Moses and other sources about joint responsibility do not fall to the wayside just because one is not serving in the army. A Jewish state should require those who receive IDF exemptions to perform national or civil service for an equal period of time. Those who do so should be recognized as having served the state and should receive the benefits that come from such recognition. In addition, most of Israel agrees that a small, select, and elite group of scholars who are completely and totally dedicated to Torah learning could actually study Torah as their national service since their complete devotion to study today will enable them to serve as guiding Torah leaders in the future. David Ben-Gurion, Israel's first prime minister, saw the need for such a group in a Jewish state and his ideal remains consistent with the teachings quoted above as long as this group is chosen and monitored based on clear parameters. (I certainly believe that the institutions where these elite scholars study should arrange for them to also be involved in community service, *hesed*, opportunities to round out their development as spiritual leaders.) These ideals form the framework for the legislation authored by my party regarding equality in national service.

The mantra repeated over and over to defend the mass exemptions from army service is the protection that Torah study provides the Jewish people and the country as well as the contribution this study makes toward national prosperity. Studying Torah, the argument goes, is actually the national service for ultra-Orthodox young men. This explanation almost always continues with the clarification that those who do not share the ultra-Orthodox belief in the power of Torah learning simply cannot relate to the degree of national service they provide through their Torah study and therefore the conversation should end there. No one has the right to even think of tampering with this aspect of their lifestyle.

I must share a critical reality with everyone who promotes and accepts this defense. The religious Zionist world shares the "Haredi belief" in the power of Torah learning. The yeshiva world in the Diaspora does, as well. But not at the cost of ignoring all else. The religious Zionist and Diaspora yeshiva worlds understand what the Israeli ultra-Orthodox world refuses to acknowledge – that one can believe in the primacy of Torah scholarship and produce the greatest Torah scholars while also spending time on other significant pursuits.

The notion that 60,000 young men need to focus exclusively on Torah study without receiving a general education, going to work, or serving in the army, in order to maintain the Torah's protection of Israel, is ludicrous. Is the Torah study of thousands of young men in the religious Zionist *hesder* yeshiva world which combines Torah study and army service not providing that protection? Is the Torah study of ultra-Orthodox IDF soldiers in Nahal Haredi and the Shahar program, where they have actual Torah classes on their bases, not providing that protection? Is the Torah study of students in Machon Lev, where they study Torah in the morning and attend university classes in the afternoon, not providing this protection? Is the Torah study of tens of thousands who learn in the early morning before going to work, on the train on the way to work, or in the late night hours after work, not providing this protection?

In addition, let's not forget about the few thousand elite scholars focusing exclusively on Torah study, as mentioned above. Most Israeli citizens want to support them so they can truly focus on their Torah study. Think about the "Torah protection" that quality of study will provide.

Imagine if the ultra-Orthodox world in Israel opened itself to army service – perhaps even "Haredi *hesder yeshivot*." I have been working with ultra-Orthodox rabbis to establish *yeshivot* which will teach the students technological skills and provide a framework for them to serve in the IDF while in a yeshiva framework. The only thing stopping these brave ultra-Orthodox rabbis from succeeding and preventing their courageous and committed students from flourishing has been past governments caving to the fear of the ultra-Orthodox political parties who don't want these institutions to receive government funding. Now, our government will rally behind these and other similar programs and we will begin to see tens of thousands of young ultra-Orthodox Torah scholars serving in the IDF, and perhaps even rise to the level of officers, while continuing to study and pray with regularity as built into the schedule of their army programs. We will still have the "protection of Torah" from the thousands studying in these and other *yeshivot*, and the Torah world would then actually have a tangible impact on the rest of the country. In addition, much of Israel's religious-secular strife would disappear.

I was studying in a yeshiva in Israel in January 1991 when Saddam Hussein threatened to attack Israel with chemical weapons. Thousands of students from the Diaspora fled Israel to the safety of their home countries. I told my parents, who left the choice up to me, that I could not imagine leaving Israel and fellow Israelis in their time of danger and made the difficult decision to remain, a decision which meant being issued my gas mask. A few weeks after that decision, I found myself, as one of the directors of the yeshiva's sealed room, waking up to a wailing air raid siren at 2:30 a.m., verifying that all of the students entered the room and then physically sealing the room.

Going to sleep every night knowing that we could be awakened to air raid sirens and the prospect of chemical attacks was frightening and unsettling. Thank God, the attacks were never chemical and caused relatively minor damage in Israel, a miracle considering the fact that thirty-nine missiles fell inside the country. But, the experience of living in such danger and sharing such deep emotions which created the deepest of bonds with my fellow Israelis, demonstrated to me how much shared difficult and even life-threatening experiences create the closest of connections and break down all barriers.

I conclude this chapter with a beautiful description of a scene which took place in 1948 on the night after Israel was declared a state, as captured by Yehuda Avner in his book, *The Prime Ministers*:

> There were about twenty-five of us, armed with pickaxes, shovels, and a dozen World War I Lee Enfield Rifles – an untrained, inglorious bucket brigade of diggers and hackers fortifying a narrow sector of Jerusalem's western front. . . . We'd heard that Iraqi irregulars were infiltrating Ein Karem to join up with a Jordanian brigade coming up from Jericho. We were supposed to stop them. . . . Grimy exhausted diggers assembled in the glow of a hurricane lamp hanging on the door of a stone ruin, hidden from enemy view, to recite the Sabbath prayers. . . .

Someone then came and told them that Ben-Gurion had declared the new state that afternoon.

> "Let's drink to that," said Elisha with delight breaking open the new bottle of wine and filling a tin mug to the brim. "A l'chayim to our new State, whatever its name!" "Wait!" shouted a chasid whom everybody knew as Nussen . . . a most diligent volunteer digger from Meah Shearim, the ultra-Orthodox area of Jerusalem. "It's Shabbos. Kiddush first." Our crowd gathered around him in a hush . . . he added the triumphantly exulted festival blessing [*shehechiyanu*] to

commemorate this first day of independence – Blessed are You, Lord our God, King of the Universe, who has given us life, sustained us, and brought us to this time. "Amen!"

Secular soldiers, religious Zionist soldiers, and ultra-Orthodox soldiers unified as Jews around a common cause – defending one another, their country, and their religion. I hope that all Jews will work together towards a return to the ideals captured in that anecdote which exhibit the true essence and values of Judaism. I am proud that our government is taking action and legislating changes in this area. Aside from the inherent benefits of our acting according to our core values, all Jews working together for the country will mitigate extremist tendencies and generate the highest levels of unity.

→ *Eight* ←

Honesty, Integrity, and the Rule of Law

MOST PEOPLE ASK THEMSELVES the following question at some point in life: "What does God expect from us? What should our focus be in life?" The Talmud (*Shabbat* 31a) asks this question in a different form – what questions will a person have to answer before God following their death? The first item on the list, the number one issue which concerns God after one passes away according to our tradition, is whether one acted with honesty in business dealings. Honesty and integrity is what is expected of us above all else. The Bible says to "stay far away from falsehood" (Exodus 23:7) and the Talmud explains that God "hates" those who lie (*Sotah* 42a).

Clearly, being honest and truthful people is a core Jewish value around which all Jews should and can unite. This ideal relates closely to another issue.

There are many impressions of my time in the former Soviet Union which I will never forget. The complete abandonment of rule of law is high on the list of those memories. I was there immediately after the fall of the Soviet Union when anarchy reigned in many of the newly formed countries. People could do whatever they wanted to do. We needed to bribe our way onto our flight from Moscow to Tbilisi because the airline ticket agents arbitrarily rejected our tickets. (We were prepped for this beforehand and brought along make-up and cigarettes to present to the individuals who stood between us and getting onto the flight.) Policemen who pulled over drivers were easily bought off with a few rubles and, as a result, everyone ignored traffic lights.

One morning a boy arrived at our camp crying. I asked him what happened and he related that as they approached their car to drive to camp, masked gunmen shot his father in the legs and stole the car. His mother called the police, but they never arrived. The father was hospitalized and the gunmen had nothing to fear.

Lawlessness is the most destructive force in the world. It is no wonder that *Ethics of Our Fathers* teaches: "Pray for the welfare of the kingdom, for if things are not stable, people will swallow each other up." I experienced this firsthand in Moscow and Tbilisi. When I saw the complete breakdown of the rule of law, I understood why, according to our tradition, setting up a system of laws and a judicial system was among the first seven laws for all mankind.

Two thousand years of diaspora life have eroded our faith in Gentile governments. However, we are still bound by the tenet that the Talmudic sage, Samuel, referred to as "The law of the land is the law." This became codified as part of Jewish law and remains in place unless a law is passed which directly contradicts Jewish law. Just to make it clear. This means that being a law abiding citizen is not simply a "civic duty" but, for the religiously observant, it becomes "a religious obligation." There were certain circumstances when the rabbis permitted local Jews to ignore or avoid obeying certain laws when they were deemed unfair and hard on the Jews, like the anti-Semitic decrees of the Russian Czars. However, those were very specific circumstances and cannot be applied today.

It is critical to remember the important role our relationship with non-Jewish leaders and governments has always played. A glance at the traditional Torah reading on Rosh Hashanah demonstrates this point. The reading on the first day of the holiday relates to the birth of Isaac and his struggles with Ishmael. That, in and of itself, places the issue of our relationships with other nations to the fore. But, then, we continue and focus on Abraham's relationship and pact with Abimelech, a Gentile king of a nearby land. Why do we focus on this on Rosh Hashanah, the new year and day of judgment? Clearly, establishing good relations with non-Jewish leaders and nations is an important Jewish value. This should most certainly negate any thoughts of violating laws because we think we need not respect non-Jewish governments.

Ironically, some view the situation in which we live today in which half of the world's Jewish population lives under the rule of a Jewish government as an excuse for violating this principle. This most certainly goes against the spirit of our tradition. How can there be any doubt that the principle of "the law of the land is the law" would apply to a Jewish government in Israel, regardless of the religious level of that government?

This relates to the core value of honesty because one area where some seem to feel very lax in obeying government laws is in the realm of taxes. A few quotes from prominent Jewish sources should put that issue to rest:

Nahmanides, a leading medieval scholar (thirteenth century Spain and Israel, also a physician):

> By living in a particular country, you implicitly agree to be
> obligated in that country's tax system, even though there is
> no signed contract.

The great fourteenth-century Talmudic commentator, Rabbi
Nissim of Gerona, Catalonia (who was also a physician and
astronomer):

> Paying taxes is like paying rent. It is the cost you incur for
> being allowed to live in a particular country and derive the
> benefits from living there.

Finally, Rabbi Moshe Isserles, the greatest authority on Ashkenazic Jewish law in sixteenth-century Poland, wrote:

> The law of the land is the law that obligates a person to
> proactively pay their taxes even if they know they won't be
> caught for failing to report income. Because fair taxation is
> an obligation that an individual takes upon himself by living
> in a country.

The bottom line is that we do not have to like or support every
government, but we are bound, nonetheless, to adhere to the
laws and pray for its welfare. As Tevya so poignantly declared
in Fiddler on the Roof, "May God bless and keep the Czar . . .
far away from us!"

Aside from the impropriety of Jews not following the law,
it actually hurts the status of Jews worldwide and leads to
anti-Semitism. This is especially true when our violations are
made public. While the Bernie Madoff scandal is certainly not
a typical situation, the reactions from the public in various pe-
riodicals in the wake of his March 2009 conviction are certainly
instructive of the damage done when Jews are not upstanding

citizens and violate laws. (Please keep in mind that these were the hateful and anti-Semitic comments which successfully made it through the website monitoring systems before they were caught and removed.)

Example from *The Washington Post* website:

> The Jewish people have got to ask themselves, now or later, how come people detest them so often. I do not. But, this is why. They are all about money, greed, selfishness, ego-centrism, showing off, being in the limelight, making more money, scratching the back of fellow Jews and so on. MONEY MONEY MONEY = Jewish culture.

Example from *The New York Times* website:

> Wah wah wah. So a bunch of rich people who are more loyal to Israel than to America lost money as a result of their greed. Who cares? I say we deport him to his brothers in Israel.

Example from *Newsweek* website:

> You people (Jews) are so pathetic and incredibly wrapped up in your self-importance. The problem must be with the way you are raised. You are coddled over and told in some way that you are very special and very important; then comes the kicker, you believe it and carry it with you into adulthood . . . Bernie Madoff sent much of his money to Israel like a good American . . . cough! Jews are loyal to themselves and to Israel in that order. They use other countries to feed that cause. If the US were to be in a war with Israel how many Jews would fight for the USA? The answer is very few. . . . Jews, the bottom line is this. You are a people who refuse to assimilate and try to change the ideals and ethos of the people who have helped you by welcoming you in their native lands . . .

Example from *The Huffington Post* website:

> Madoff stole $60 billion dollars and shipped it to Israel. Jewish Talmudic law states that a Jew can steal from the subhuman (*goyim*) and it's legal to do.

Example from *The Independent* website in England:

> I don't know what all the fuss is about. The greedy Jew fleeced other greedy Jews & the "Jewish economy" is minus a few billion dollars. The greedy ones went to Madoff who was even more greedier and the whole thing became a dog's breakfast and they all got well & truly fleeced. Simple. A well-deserved self-inflicted financial holocaust. So there you are.

We have enough enemies without trying to arouse hate from those around us. Aside from the core value of following the law of the land, violating the laws does terrible damage to fellow Jews and to our general standing throughout the world.

I was blessed to grow up in a family with a father who was a federal judge. The entire family culture was adhering to the laws of the land and a tremendous appreciation for all that our country does for us. I mentioned earlier in the book that we are called Jews, *Yehudim*, based on the root "*hodah*", which means "thank you." We must be a people who recognize the good that has been done to us by others since that is supposed to be our very essence. Living in a land that provides our basic needs warrants allegiance and observance of the laws of the land.

This value is one which all Jews must unite around. Following the rule of law and living with the highest levels of honesty and integrity are important Jewish values which we must work to restore in all our populations as we strive to become a true "light unto the nations."

⇶ *Nine* ⇜

The Bible

ATTENDING THE NATIONAL PRAYER BREAKFAST in Washington as one of the proud representatives of Israel, I was moved deeply when President Obama declared, "I wake up every morning and spend a little time in scripture . . . and I must make sure that those values motivate me." As I reflected upon what he said, I suddenly remembered another powerful scene in my life. A number of years ago, I served as the head counselor in a Jewish sports camp. One morning, I woke up very early and decided to go for a jog. As I walked down the hallway I saw our head basketball coach, a Christian, sitting and reading. I was shocked. After all, it was 6:00 a.m. As I approached Coach, he looked up and said, "That's right. To be a better basketball coach I need to start my day early with some lessons from the Bible."

People around the world recognize the benefit which comes from regular Bible study. Jews have always been known as "the People of the Book." While there is no question we have always had high percentages of literacy throughout the ages, "the book" refers to one book and one book only – the Bible. And we need to get back to using it as a resource in our lives. The Bible's stories and teachings contain lessons and values for all areas of life and it should serve as a guiding and unifying force for Jews around the world.

There are many memorable moments from my first few months in the Knesset but one which stands out was MK Dr. Ruth Calderon's inaugural address. I saw Ruth stand up with her Talmud in hand, and turned to a fellow MK sitting next to me and said, "Watch this. This is going to be special." Sure enough, Ruth taught a section of the Talmud with clarity and in-depth insights. There was a buzz in the Knesset and the video of her speech went viral. Ruth is not "religious." But she showed that Torah belongs to all of us and it is something which all Jews can connect to.

Tuesday at 3:00 p.m. is a special time in the Knesset. MK Calderon and Education Minister Rabbi Shai Piron established a Torah study session for Knesset members and their staff. Members of the coalition and opposition, religious and not religious, men and women – we sit around a table in a Knesset committee room and discuss a passage in the Bible or the Talmud. This is a precious part of the week for all of us. Aside from the fact that it enables us to pause from the hectic Knesset schedule to focus on spirituality and remind us why we are here and what a Jewish country is all about, we all unite around the source of all Jewish values and ideals.

The Bible provides us with lessons about the importance of family, how to succeed in relationships, proper parenting, the pitfalls of pursing honor, the dangers of jealousy, the fleeting nature and damage which comes from pursuing immoral physical desires, and more.

I encourage parents to sit and read the Bible with their children and to discuss its eternal messages. In addition, all Jewish schools from the most religious to the most secular should "get back to the basics" and study the Bible from cover to cover, and teachers should generate lively discussions among the students and empower them to draw life lessons from our rich heritage.

As we move forward towards reconnecting to what it means to be Jews, familiarizing ourselves with the Bible and its wealth of lessons and values will enable it to continue serving as the unifying force it has been for the Jewish people throughout the generations.

⇾ *Ten* ⇽

Jewish Pride

IT WAS A VERY poignant moment. I sat down to have lunch with a Christian colleague at the kosher pizza shop in Silver Spring, Maryland. I went to the sink to ritually wash my hands and then quickly mumbled a blessing before taking a bite out of my pizza. I am not certain if my colleague saw me do this or not, but he asked me if I minded if he said grace before we ate. He then went on to recite a beautiful blessing, proudly embracing his faith. I felt so small and realized that if I had truly felt proud of being Jewish, the way my colleague felt proud to be Christian, I would not have played down my rituals in that manner.

The time has come for all Jews to live with open Jewish pride. We have so much to make us feel proud. The starting point for that pride must be all the values in this book. If we truly live our lives by these most basic ideals, we will be the most upstanding, decent, and contributing nation on the planet, filled to the brim with reasons to walk around as proud Jews.

The truth is that pride in our contribution to the world should already exist. Jews make up just a quarter of one percent of the world's population yet they have won 177 Nobel prizes, which amounts to 18% of the total awarded. Jews have won these prizes in all fields – literature, chemistry, physiology/medicine, physics, peace, and economics.

The world is a different and much better place today because of Jewish inventions and ideas. The list of modern-day technologies and conveniences which Jews have been instrumental in bringing into the world is long, but here is a brief list: cell phones, Pentium MMX chip technology, voice mail technology, instant messenger, Google, and Facebook. Think about how different our world is because of the technological contributions.

Aside from the impact on communication and the realm of convenience technology, Jews have made major breakthroughs in the world of medicine. Jews are responsible for: the first fully computerized, no radiation diagnostic instrumentation for breast cancer; the first ingestible video camera fit into a pill and used to view the small intestine from the inside to help diagnose cancer and other diseases; a new device that directly helps the heart pump blood which can save lives of those with heart failure; treatment to enable women who have undergone chemotherapy to give birth through a transplant of ovarian tissue; the development of a method to use the blood of a newborn's umbilical cord as a resource for stem cells that can be injected into a heart to regenerate damaged heart tissue; development of human stem cells to treat different neurological disorders and central nervous system traumas; treatment for strokes with reduced side effects; the creation of a new saliva test for hepatitis C which will make testing easier and more widespread, and containment and treatment much more effective; the discovery of the molecular trigger that causes psoriasis; the invention of the "ex-press shunt" which provides relief for those who suffer from glaucoma; the creation of "bone glue" which will reduce the need for bone transplants; the development of the use of elderberry, one of the best-selling flu prevention medicines; the discovery that chemicals in snake venom can serve as a powerful analgesic for the relief of chronic pain of arthritis and even cancer; and the creation of "clear light" which causes acne bacteria to self-destruct without damaging surrounding skin. All of these recent medical advances were achieved by Jews in Israel alone.

If we shift to the overall topic of this book, basic values and Israel, the Jewish country stands out in many ways. Israel is the only liberal democracy in the Middle East. As was referenced in the book, Israel airlifted 22,000 Ethiopian Jews who were at risk in Ethiopia in 1984 and 1991 and brought them home to safety in Israel. Golda Meir became Israel's Prime Minister in 1969, making her the second female in modern times to hold a country's highest office. Israeli rescue teams saved three victims from the rubble of the bombed United States Embassy in Nairobi in 1998 – arriving on the scene within a day of the attack. Israel is the largest immigrant-absorbing country on earth when viewed in terms of its overall population. On the environmental front, Israel is the only country in the world that entered the twenty-first century with a net gain of trees. An Israeli company developed and installed the first large-scale solar-powered and fully functional electricity generating plant.

Our pride should be magnified knowing that we have been able to accomplish this much and more, and that we contribute so much to the world despite all the persecution we have experienced. Mark Twain captured it best. He wrote the following in *Harper's Magazine* in 1899:

If the statistics are right, the Jews constitute but one quarter of one percent of the human race. It suggests a nebulous puff of star dust lost in the blaze of the Milky Way. Properly, the Jew ought hardly to be heard of, but he is heard of, has always been heard of. He is as prominent on the planet as any other people, and his importance is extravagantly out of proportion to the smallness of his bulk.

His contributions to the world's list of great names in literature, science, art, music, finance, medicine, and abstruse learning are also very out of proportion to the weakness of his numbers. He has made a marvelous fight in this world in all ages; and has done it with his hands tied behind him. He could be vain of himself and be excused for it. The Egyptians, the Babylonians, and the Persians rose, filled the planet with sound and splendor, then faded to dream-stuff and passed away; the Greeks and Romans followed and made a vast noise, and they were gone; other people have sprung up and held their torch high for a time but it burned out, and they sit in twilight now, and have vanished.

The Jew saw them all, survived them all, and is now what he always was, exhibiting no decadence, no infirmities of age, no weakening of his parts, no slowing of his energies, no dulling of his alert but aggressive mind. All things are mortal but the Jews; all other forces pass, but he remains.

I had the great honor of participating in a remarkable rally in Bet Shemesh, which I alluded to in the introduction, and which I will expound upon in the next chapter. That rally, which included thousands of Jews from all over Israel, was covered on national television. I spoke about my love for all of my fellow Jews regardless of their affiliation and how we need to work together to make our country great.

The next night I took my wife out to dinner and a non-religious waiter in his mid-twenties approached our table. He told me that he saw me on television the night before and then he said words which sent shivers up and down my spine:

> Seeing you on the stage, clearly a very Orthodox Jew from the way you dress, saying that you love all Jews and we can work together, it was the first time in my life that I felt proud to be a Jew.

As I traveled around Israel during the election campaign, I repeatedly heard the same sad statement from young, secular Israelis: "I hate Judaism, and I hate that I hate Judaism." How can it be that young Israelis "hate" Judaism? How could it be that the young waiter had never felt proud to be Jewish? We must change that. The time has come for all Jews to reach deep inside and bring back Jewish pride. All of the topics in the earlier chapters certainly provide the basis for it. Now we have to make it happen because we are losing our people. Inter-marriage rates are approaching 50%. Jews around the world need a reason to want to remain identified with the Jewish people. Embracing the perspectives, ideals, and values outlined in this book will help redefine and unite us as one nation and can serve as the key towards restoring much needed and very well-justified Jewish pride.

⇢ *Eleven* ⇠

Unity

The city of Bet Shemesh made international headlines at the end of 2011. The story went public when 8-year old Naama Margolese was seen on television crying because religious extremists made going to and from school a daily nightmare. Most people do not realize that this was not a one-time event, but something that transpired over the course of months. Adults from the neighborhood patrolled the streets on a daily basis in order to protect the girls.

On the first really difficult day, when the extremists were especially vicious in their screams of "stop defiling our neighborhood" and "*prutza*" (literally, "immodest one" with a connotation of "prostitute") towards the little girls, the extremists actually turned on me. They surrounded me, were poking at me, spat at me, and called me "Satan" and "Nazi." Every fiber of my being wanted to lunge at them and fight back. But, something deep inside of me told me that the last thing we can allow is a civil war in the streets of Bet Shemesh. This guided our approach as a community through the entire saga.

The intimidation and assaults on the girls quieted for some

time, but the extremists returned and it was clear something drastic needed to be done to stop them. We made the decision to turn to the Israeli press. This led to a series of interviews throughout the city which aired on national television. After the program aired I received an e-mail from a friend which included a link and a message, "Did you see this Facebook group?" I clicked on the link and panicked when I saw its name: "Thousands of Israelis going to Bet Shemesh to protect little Naama." I could not believe my eyes. Thousands of Israelis wanted to march through the extremist neighborhood with torches. I felt I had the duty to stop this before it led to Jews fighting against Jews in my own city.

It took me some time, but I eventually reached the group administrator. I tried to convince the group to change their plans since this did not really fit into what we had in mind, but then a young, non-religious Israeli said words which I will never forget. He said, "Dov, I was sitting in my home minding my own business, surfing the channels, when all of a sudden I saw a little Jewish girl crying because she felt unsafe going to and from school. No one will stop me from doing something for that girl." I was touched so deeply by his response and agreed to work together to hold some form of protest in Bet Shemesh.

Sure enough, over the course of the next few days I found myself working together with leaders of groups that I had always viewed with great negativity. Organizations such as *Yisrael Chofshit* (Free Israel) and *Hit'orerut Yerushalayim* (Wake up Jerusalem) were always portrayed to me as very secular and perhaps even anti-religious. They certainly appeared to be radically left-wing politically. Meeting with the heads of these groups was extremely eye-opening for me. While we may disagree about many things, I learned that these were beautiful Jews who were trying to do what they thought was best for

Judaism. And, most importantly, they were not anti-religious. Like most people, they just don't want to be told what to do.

So, we set aside our disagreements and found unity in many areas of agreement – no extremism, no religious coercion, and certainly no violence. Several nights later we declared this message before thousands of Israelis who attended the rally and to the tens of thousands who were watching it live on Israeli television. Sure enough, that was all it took. The extremists never came back again. The girls were safe from that day forward. We managed to avoid a civil war of any kind during those difficult months and defeated extremism through the power of our unity. We rallied the entire country against this group, and finally, they backed off.

This was a very important lesson regarding the power of our unity. I learned this same lesson again seven months later when I had the privilege to be a part of the rally in Tel Aviv demanding equality in national service. As I spoke to the crowd of over 40,000 people, I looked out and saw Jews from all walks of life who put aside political, ideological, and theological differences to unite around an issue about which we all agreed – that every citizen should serve the country in army or national service. The Prime Minister had no choice but to address the demands of the protestors and historic legislation is being passed.

I learned this lesson one more time during the election campaign of 2012. I joined the Yesh Atid party led by now Finance Minister Yair Lapid, who gathered people from all backgrounds to form his list for Knesset. For two months, male, female, religious, secular, Ashkenazic, Sephardic, Ethiopian, Russian, and English-speaking candidates traveled around the country talking about our message of putting aside our differences and working together. And the country responded in the voting booth, sending nineteen of us to the Knesset.

The importance of unifying around a common goal is beautifully portrayed in the story of my son's experience on the Israel national little league baseball team. Fifteen 11- and 12-year olds were chosen to represent Israel as part of an international tournament in Italy where Israel had never previously won a baseball tournament at any level. At first glance this team seemed doomed for failure simply based on the players' backgrounds. In a country polarized by ideological boxes how could this group possibly succeed? The team was comprised of non-observant boys from secular kibbutzim, boys with national religious backgrounds, and even boys from more ultra-Orthodox leaning schools. Since unity is required to produce the teamwork necessary to win at all levels, on paper this team seemed bound to repeat Israel's previous failures at baseball tournaments abroad.

However, something remarkable happened. As practice began, these children saw beyond the boxes into which we, adults, had painted them. It didn't matter to them whether another boy wore a *kippah*; they were Jews playing for Israel. Among those who wore *kippot* it was irrelevant to any of them whether one was wearing knit, leather, or black velvet; they were Jews playing for Israel. It didn't concern them that some boys had long hair and others long sidelocks, Hassidic style. They were a team. They were playing with "Israel" sewn across the front of their jerseys. They were Jews. They were unified as one.

Once all the labels and barriers were put aside, they went to Italy, dominated their games, and returned to Israel with the gold medal. Fifteen Israeli boys went to Europe and stood proudly in their blue and white uniforms and held a large, Israeli flag as they were presented with the first place trophy. They were champions. These children teach us how much we can accomplish if we would simply set aside our differences and unite as the Jewish people and as citizens of Israel, regardless of how we look externally and our level of religious observance.

The Bible records that the Jews were camped around Mount Sinai and the Talmud expounds that they were "like one person with one heart." But, then, as they traveled from Sinai, the Bible describes how each tribe had its own flag and special place to camp. Why were we creating such divisions after that massive show of unity at Sinai?

The answer is clear. Unity does not mean that we agree about everything. We are going to be different as demonstrated by the different tribes and their individual flags. Unity means treating each other with basic respect despite our differences, and putting aside those differences in order to work together when we can. In the desert it was reflected by the rituals in the Tabernacle which sat in the middle of the camp, in Bet Shemesh it meant resisting religious coercion, and, in Tel Aviv, it meant demanding equality and fairness. In each of these cases, the highest levels of unity were on display despite the significant ideological chasms between the groups.

I have been blessed with the opportunity to feel this sense of unity with fellow Israelis. This was most dramatic during times of war, with campers and their parents in Tbilisi, with Ethiopian Jews upon their arrival in Israel, and with Ethiopians in Gondar who were awaiting permission to immigrate to Israel. There was a natural bond that we all felt towards one another despite our differences. Morrie Schwartz, the professor dying of Lou Gehrig's disease in *Tuesdays with Morrie*, told the story of "The Wave:"

> The waves were all out in the ocean bobbing up and down and having a great time. Suddenly, one of the waves said, "Why are we having fun? This is crazy. All the waves are crashing

into the beach and disappearing. All is lost!" Another wave responded to him, "You are looking at this all wrong. We aren't individual waves. We are part of the ocean. . . ."

All Jews are part of a unique ocean. As the Mark Twain quote in the previous chapter captured so poignantly, we are on a national journey together. Every generation plays its role with different challenges and circumstances. But we share the deepest of bonds regardless of those differences in geography, culture, and even beliefs.

Let us all commit to setting aside our differences to unite around the core values which make us one. The time has come for all of us – male, female, young, old, religious, and not religious – to reaffirm what it means to be Jews with the restoration of a moderate, embracing, value-centered, and unified Judaism. If we follow the steps outlined throughout this book and unify as a nation, we will have done what is absolutely necessary to save our nation.